W0417181

JENNIFER GALLAGHER

The Tail of Sherlock Bones

CORNELSEN ENGLISH LIBRARY

Cornelsen

Cornelsen English Library

Verlagsredaktion
Nathalie Schwering

Umschlaggestaltung
hawemannundmosch, Konzeption und Gestaltung, Berlin

Bildquellen
mauritius images, Mittenwald: Alamy/Barrie Harwood Photography (Titelbild); Photolibrary, London (ch. 1, p. 13: Sodapix AG / Zumbrunn Michel); istockPhoto, Calgary (ch. 2, p. 25: Andy Gehrig; ch. 4, p. 47, ch. 8, p. 83: Achim Prill); Boston (ch. 3); Cinetext, Frankfurt / Main (ch. 5, p. 53: Concorde); © 2009 Greater Boston Convention and Visitors Bureau; Heimat für Tiere – Neue Zeit e. V., Birkenfeld (ch. 6, p. 64); Jule Pfeiffer-Spiekermann, Freising (ch. 6, p. 64 (Wiese), 7, p. 75 (Wasser), 8, p. 83 (Landeplatz, Weg), 9, p. 96 (Bildschirm)); Shutterstock, New York (ch. 7, p. 75: Botond Horváth)

Illustration
Jule Pfeiffer-Spiekermann, Freising

Gestaltung & technische Umsetzung
Annika Preyhs für Buchgestaltung+, Berlin

www.cornelsen.de

1. Auflage, 3. Druck 2015

Alle Drucke dieser Auflage sind inhaltlich unverändert und können im Unterricht nebeneinander verwendet werden.

Druck: Offizin Andersen Nexö Leipzig

ISBN 978-3-06-032301-2

Inhalt gedruckt auf säurefreiem Papier aus nachhaltiger Forstwirtschaft.

Contents

For my dog Wellington,
(October 11, 1981 to July 26, 1997)
who gave me most of the ideas for this story.

Chapter 1 A royal start

Max opened one of his eyes and saw two big black eyes looking back at him. The eyes belonged to Sherlock, who was Max's dog. Sherlock was a big Old English sheepdog. Actually, he wasn't old. He was about four, but he was very big.

"It's still early, Sherlock. I don't have to get up yet, there's no school for another week. Go and lie down and let me sleep a bit more," grumbled Max.

But Sherlock didn't lie down. He wanted Max to get up. It was true: it was still the school holidays, but this was the day that Max and his mother, Mrs Bradley, were going to drive to Scotland from their flat in London for a few days and Sherlock was going with them.

There was only one way to really wake up Max, and Sherlock knew how to do it. He suddenly jumped onto Max's bed with a big crash!

"Get off, you big elephant!" shouted Max. "What's the matter with you? You know that you're not allowed on the bed. You'll break it. You've already broken the sofa. If you break anything else, Mum will get really angry and take you to the dog rescue centre."

Max pushed Sherlock off the bed and Sherlock fell onto the floor with the sound of an even bigger crash.

"What's going on up there?" shouted Mrs Bradley from the kitchen.

"Nothing, Mum, I ... er ... fell out of bed," Max shouted back.

"How can somebody fall out of bed? I'm sure Sherlock made that noise," shouted Mrs Bradley from downstairs.

Max looked at Sherlock. "See? Try to stay out of trouble," whispered Max. Sherlock looked at Max, put his head on his big paws and moved his tail very slowly from side to side.

Max's mother shouted from the kitchen again. "Please get up and come downstairs, Max. Breakfast is ready. We have to leave soon and you have to take Sherlock for a walk. It's a long drive to Scotland!"

Max got out of bed and sat on the floor. He put his head in his hands. Max had forgotten that he was going to Scotland with his mother. Mrs Bradley was a photographer and had to take photos at the Edinburgh Fringe Festival for a magazine. How boring. Max wanted to stay at home in London and hang out with his mates.

"Well, at least you're coming to Scotland so I'll have somebody to talk to," Max said to Sherlock, who was sitting next to him on the floor. The big dog wagged his tail madly and licked Max's face all over.

"Yuck, now my face is all wet, you silly dog," said Max.

Max quickly got dressed and opened his bedroom door. "OK. Let's have breakfast, I'm starving."

As soon as Max said the word 'breakfast' Sherlock ran out of Max's room and downstairs towards the kitchen like a fast train.

"Not so fast, you crazy dog!" shouted Max. "Wait for me."

As Sherlock ran into the kitchen, Mrs Bradley was coming out and almost fell over him.

"Get out of my way, Sherlock! Why do we have such a big dog?" she said to herself. "Most people have small dogs that sleep all day."

Max came running down the stairs.

"Can't you control your dog?" said Mrs Bradley. "I almost broke my neck!"

"I'm really sorry, Mum," said Max. "I told Sherlock to wait but…"

"Telling a big dog like Sherlock to wait isn't enough," said Mrs Bradley angrily. "He needs to go to a dog school, or be given to somebody who can control him. Now, please give him some breakfast before he eats the kitchen table, and then put him outside in the back yard."

A few minutes later, Max and his mother were sitting at the table eating breakfast in silence until Max said:

"Mum, do I really have to go to Edinburgh? Can't I stay at home? It's only for a couple of days."

"I don't want you to stay at home alone," answered Mrs Bradley.

"Why not?" grumbled Max. "My friends are allowed to stay alone at home while their parents go on short trips."

"I don't care what your friends are allowed to do," said Mrs Bradley.

"I'm 15. I'm not a baby," said Max.

"That's true," said Mrs Bradley. "But you'd forget to eat, or get into some kind of trouble. I would just worry about you."

"Sherlock would tell me to eat. He never forgets about food," said Max.

"You're right about that. He likes to eat sofas!" said Mrs Bradley. "If I left you two alone, there wouldn't be any furniture when I came back!"

Max looked down at his plate and didn't say anything.

"Anyway, I think it will be nice to spend some time together, don't you?" Mrs Bradley said. "I don't see much of you. You're usually in your room in front of your computer, or out with your friends and Sherlock."

Max didn't answer. He looked out of the window and saw with horror that Sherlock was looking at Mrs Bradley's favourite flowers as if he was thinking about eating them.

"Er, I'm going to take Sherlock for his long walk now," said Max.

"That's a very good idea, he needs a good run. Make sure you're back here by 11 o'clock," said Mrs Bradley.

"OK, Mum," said Max.

He went outside into the yard to get Sherlock and saw that Mrs Bradley's favourite plant was still in one piece. This is going to be a horrible journey. I hate Scotland already, Max thought to himself.

Max thought about where he could take Sherlock for a long walk. Although there was a small park near to where Max lived, Max thought that Hyde Park would be the best – it was the biggest park in London. Big dogs like big parks! But how was he going to get to Hyde Park? A bus would take too long. The best and quickest way to get there was by car. His best mate Zack had a car and maybe Zack could pick them up and drive them there.

Max took his mobile phone from his pocket. Sherlock jumped up and tried to take the phone.

"Get down, Sherlock. This is a mobile phone, not a dog biscuit," laughed Max as he started to write a text message to Zack:

SOS can u take me+Sherl 2 Hyde Park?

Max clicked on 'send' and looked at his watch. When had Mum told him to be back home? Had she said 11 or 12?

His phone beeped. It was Zack's answer:

OK when?

Max sent another text to Zack:

Now! Meet on corner bring car

Again, Max's mobile beeped:

C U in 10 mins

Exactly ten minutes later, Zack arrived in his red Mini. He opened the car door.

"Get in mate," said Zack.

Max pushed Sherlock into the back of Zack's Mini and got in the front. Then Zack drove off quickly.

"Thanks for picking us up," said Max.

"No worries. So, er... what's going on? What's with the SOS?" asked Zack. "You look a bit fed up."

Max told Zack about the trip to Scotland with his mother, and how he couldn't think of anything worse. Just then a traffic light turned red and Zack had to stop.

"There are things much worse than that," said Zack. "Look at that man who's sleeping on that bench over there. He doesn't have a home and he probably doesn't know where his next meal is coming from."

Max didn't say anything. The light turned green and a few minutes later they were driving over Waterloo Bridge and towards the London Eye. He looked out of the car window and saw the boats sail up and down the River Thames.

Zack drove past the Houses of Parliament and Big Ben. Just then, Sherlock put his head on Max's shoulder and burped loudly in his ear.

"Yuck, that smells really bad," said Max, and he opened the window.

"I'll open my window, too. It smells like bad eggs in here," said Zack.

"Sorry, mate," said Max to his friend.

"No worries. We'll be in the park soon," said Zack.

About ten minutes later they drove past Buckingham Palace where the Queen lives when she is in London.

"It's strange to think that the Queen lives in that big palace," said Max. "I've never seen her, have you?"

"I've only seen her on TV and in Madame Tussauds. I've never seen her walking about in London or anything like that," said Zack.

"I don't really care about the Queen," said Max. "What's she got to do with me…?"

"Yeah, I know what you mean. But she likes dogs. I read in a magazine that she's got about 12," said Zack. "They probably wear dog collars that have diamonds in them."

"Don't let Sherlock hear that. He might want a collar with jewels," said Max. "He's just got one with his name and my mobile phone number on it if he gets lost. I wonder if any of the Queen's dogs ever get lost."

"If somebody found one of her dogs, they would sell the collar with all those jewels in it, and ask the Queen for a lot of money or they would kill the dog," said Zack.

"That's terrible," said Max.

"Well, about 600 dogs are stolen in the UK every day," said Zack.

"What! How do you know that?" asked Max.

"I read about it on the BBC website. Dog thieves sell dogs to get money for drugs. It's a big business. So keep an eye on Sherlock!"

"He never leaves my side," said Max. "A dog thief has to kill me before they steal Sherlock!"

"Well, let's hope nothing like that happens," said Max.

A few minutes later Max, Zack and Sherlock were in Hyde Park. There were lots of people in the park because the sun was shining. The two boys walked towards a big lake and Sherlock ran in front of them chasing the birds on the grass.

"How long is the drive to Edinburgh?" asked Max.

"Hmmm, about seven hours, I think," said Zack.

"Seven hours? Oh no, I didn't know that it was that long," said Max. "You can fly to New York from London in five hours."

"Well, at least you can stop on the way. You can't do that in a plane. The visit to Edinburgh might not be so bad. I've heard it's a cool city."

"Yeah, if your mother isn't with you," grumbled Max.

"Just send me an SOS if it gets really bad," laughed Zack.

"Very funny," said Max. "But I'll take my laptop so that we can chat online. It's cheaper than sending text messages."

"OK, cool," said Zack. "Where's Sherlock? He was here a minute ago."

Max put his hand up to his eyes because the sun was so bright, and then he looked towards the lake.

"There he is," said Max, "near the water. He's running around in circles eating the bread people are throwing on the grass for the birds. Can you see him?"

"Oh, yeah, there he is. He's fast," laughed Zack. "Those birds don't have a chance to get any bread. He's like a turbo vacuum cleaner."

Just then, a little girl, who was standing at the side of the lake, threw a big piece of bread to one of the beautiful white swans that were swimming on the water. The piece of bread almost hit the big white bird on its head. Suddenly, Sherlock ran past. He wanted to get that bread! There was a loud splash as he jumped into the water and almost landed on one of the swans. The other swan flapped its wings and made loud, angry noises as Sherlock swam past its partner and tried to reach the bread that was still in the water.

"Oh, no, Sherlock almost killed a swan! I can't take my eyes off him for a minute," said Max angrily. "Sherlock, come here! Now!" he shouted to Sherlock, who was swimming to the side of the lake with the large piece of bread in his mouth. The swans swam to the other side of the lake to get away from Sherlock as quickly as they could.

"No, it's OK," said Zack. "I bet you didn't know that you could go to prison if you kill a swan because all the swans in England belong to the Queen."

"No, I didn't. Did you read that on the BBC website, too?" joked Max.

"Yep," said Zack.

A few seconds later, Sherlock was standing on the grass. He shook the water off himself.

"Let's go home before something else happens," said Max.

Sherlock and the two boys started to walk back the way they had come. Just then, as they were about to cross the only road that goes through the park, they heard the loud noise of a police siren. Suddenly a policeman on a motorbike with a flashing blue light rode up to them and stopped. He looked very serious.

"Stay where you are! Don't cross the road!" said the policeman to the boys.

"What's happening?" Max asked Zack. "Are we in trouble because Sherlock almost killed one of the Queen's birds?"

"I don't know," whispered Zack. "Don't say anything."

Suddenly two more policemen on motorbikes rode towards Sherlock and the two boys. A black car followed the two policemen. It had big windows, and a coat of arms and a flag on the top. The driver was wearing a black uniform. In the back there was just one person – a serious woman with silver hair, who looked very important. As the black car drove past, the woman looked out of the car's window. She saw Sherlock and smiled.

When the black car had passed, the policeman didn't say anything. He started his motorbike and followed the black car with his blue light still flashing.

"Wow! Amazing. Am I dreaming? That was the Queen," said Max. "She drove past right in front of us and even smiled at Sherlock."

"Yeah, that was pretty amazing," said Zack.

"I wonder where she was going," said Max.

"Maybe she's going to Balmoral Castle – that's her home in Scotland. So, you might see her again," laughed Zack.

"Scotland?" said Max. He looked at his watch. "Oh, no, I almost forgot. We have to get back.

"OK. But er... before we go, have you got a plastic bag?" asked Zack. "Sherlock has made a big mountain of dog shit – I guess the Queen didn't see it!"

When Max got home, Mrs Bradley was putting a suitcase and her camera bag into the car, which was an old Mercedes. It was so old that it didn't even have electric windows or an electronic central lock system. Mrs Bradley didn't want to sell it and get a new one because it had belonged to Mr Bradley.

"Hi, Mum," said Max.

"Ah, there you are," said Mrs Bradley as she closed the door of the car. "I was about to call the police."

"You're joking," said Max. "I'm not that late, am I?"

"No, but I called you on your mobile. I don't know why you have a mobile phone when you don't even answer it," grumbled Mrs Bradley. "But you're back now and that's the main thing," she said. "Did you have a good walk with Sherlock?"

Max thought about telling his mother that he had seen the Queen in Hyde Park but then she would want to know how he had got to Hyde Park. Mrs Bradley didn't like Max's friend Zack very much. Actually, she didn't like any of Max's friends very much. So, it was probably better not to tell her. Anyway, it was nice to have a secret.

"It was fine," said Max.

"Good," said Mrs Bradley. "Go and pack your stuff. And pack some dog food for Sherlock and lots of water for him and us. I've already made some sandwiches for us."

"Can I check my e-mails first?" asked Max.

"I don't think there's time for that," said Mrs Bradley, "we have to leave in about 30 minutes."

"Why do we have to leave so soon?" grumbled Max.

"It's a long drive, Max," said Mrs Bradley, "and it would be nice to get to Edinburgh for dinner."

Max went into the kitchen and Sherlock followed him. Mum drives me nuts, he thought to himself.

Chapter 2 Off to Scotland

Motorways are so boring. Max turned to look at Sherlock, who was asleep on the back seat. It's alright for him – it's a dog's life, he thought.

Max looked out of the car window. A road sign on the side of the motorway flashed past: "Speed kills – slow down".

Suddenly something touched his arm.

"Are you OK? What are you listening to?" asked Mrs Bradley.

Max took the headphone out of his right ear.

"Sorry, what did you say?" he said.

"What are you listening to?" she asked again.

"Er, the Red Hot Chilli Peppers," said Max.

"Ah, the vegetable band again," said Mrs Bradley.

"Yeah, it's their 'Live in Hyde Park' album. I think it's their best."

"Oh," said Mrs Bradley. "I'd like to listen to it with you – maybe in Edinburgh.

"We could but it's probably not your kind of music, Mum," said Max. He put the headphone back in his ear. His dad had liked the Chilli Peppers. They had often listened to them together.

Hours went by. Another road sign flashed past: "Tiredness kills – take a break". Just then, Sherlock stood up and touched the side of Mrs Bradley's face with his large cold nose. She screamed. It wasn't a loud scream, but it was a scream.

"Were you asleep Mum?" said Max, laughing.

"I suppose you think that's funny," Mrs Bradley said. "OK, you're right. I am a bit tired and Sherlock needs a walk and something to drink. Let's take a break soon and have something to eat."

"That's a great idea," agreed Max. "I'm starving and I'm sure Sherlock is too, and it will be good to walk around a bit."

Just then, another sign flashed past with 'Services – 5 miles' and pictures of a petrol pump, a cup and a picnic table on it.

"Perfect," smiled Mrs Bradley. "We'll get off the motorway there. Well done Sherlock."

A few minutes later Mrs Bradley parked the car near the picnic area.

"This is a nice place, isn't it?" she said. "We can have our sandwiches on a picnic table under those trees over there. It will be much cooler. I don't know about you, but I'm beginning to melt in this heat."

"Yeah, me too," said Max. "I bet Sherlock can't wait to get out of this hot car."

"Do you want to get him out of the car now, while I quickly go to the toilet," asked Mrs Bradley. "Then I'll come back and get our sandwiches out of the car and meet you at the picnic table. OK?"

"I'm dying to go to the toilet, too," said Max. "So maybe he can stay in the car just for a minute."

"That should be fine," said Mrs Bradley as she started to close her window.

"Oh, where are the sandwiches, Mum?"

"They're in the boot of the car, why?"

"Well, I don't want Sherlock to eat them while we're gone."

"Good point. I'm glad one of us is thinking straight. Oh dear, I'm more tired than I thought. I'll be back in a minute," Mrs Bradley said as she got out of the car and closed the door.

Sherlock was standing up and wagging his tail. He tried to jump into the front of the car, but Max turned to Sherlock and wouldn't let him.

"No, you wait here for a minute, Sherlock," he said as he closed his window, making sure there was a bit of space at the top so that Sherlock would have some air. "I have to go to the toilet as well. Then I'll come back and let you out."

Max got out of the car, closed his door and ran towards the toilet. But Sherlock didn't want to wait. He jumped from the back onto Max's seat and put his big front paws on the side window, and wagged his tail wildly.

A few minutes later, Max walked back to the car. He looked towards the picnic tables so see if his mum was already there with the sandwiches, but she wasn't. She must still be in the toilet, he thought.

When Max got to the car Sherlock was very happy to see him and started barking.

"OK, OK, keep your hair on," said Max, "now it's your turn."

Max tried to open the door of the car so that Sherlock could jump out but it wouldn't open. It was locked!

"Sherlock, you're an idiot, you've locked the door," he laughed.

Max went around to the driver's side of the car and tried to open that. But it was locked too.

Just then, Max saw his mum coming out of the toilet and walking towards the car.

"Mum, have you got the car keys?" Max asked her.

"Why? You didn't lock your side, did you?" she said.

"No, but Sherlock must have stood on the door lock on my side and locked the door. Your door is locked."

Mrs Bradley looked in her bag and then in the pockets of her jeans.

"The keys aren't here," she said. "Oh, no, where are they?"

"You must have locked it with the key before you went to the toilet."

"But I never lock it with the keys. The lock is a bit old and I'm always worried that I will break the key or something. I always press the door lock and then close the door. Maybe you left them in the toilet or something. They can't be far."

Just then Max looked in the car through the window on the driver's side.

"Mum, look! The keys are still inside the car!"

Mrs Bradley looked through the window.

"I don't believe it! I locked the door and left the keys in the car. How could I be so stupid? I've never done that before. I guess I'm just really tired." She put her hand over her mouth with shock.

Max was getting upset.

"The car is locked and Sherlock is inside. It's hot in there and he needs water. He could die. What are we going to do?" he shouted.

Mrs Bradley quickly took her mobile phone out of her bag.

"I'm going to call the road-help people. Good thing I brought my AA card," she said. "Don't worry, Max. They'll send somebody to open the car."

"Well, I hope they will send somebody quickly," cried Max. "It's really hot in that car although the window's open a bit."

Inside the car, Sherlock started to bark. Max put his hand against the window and tried to calm Sherlock down.

"It's OK, Sherlock. We'll get you out of there", said Max through the window.

Sherlock wagged his tail very slowly.

Max looked at his mother, who was talking to the AA on the phone. How could she be so stupid to leave the keys in the car?

He listened to what his mother was saying on the phone: "Can't you send somebody sooner?"

"Well, what did they say, Mum?" asked Max.

"It will be about two hours before they can get here," said Mrs Bradley.

"What! Two hours! Sherlock can't wait that long," cried Max angrily. "Why can't they get here sooner? This is an emergency."

He looked at Sherlock, who had stopped barking, but his long pink tongue was hanging out, and he was panting.

"They're very busy," said Mrs Bradley.

"Well, we can't just stand here and wait two hours until somebody comes to open the car."

"Maybe the police can be here faster than the AA. I'll phone them."

"I've got a better idea: why don't I break the window with a large stone?"

"Let me call the police first, Max. We might hurt Sherlock if we break the window. And breaking a car window isn't as easy as you think it is."

Max wasn't really listening to his mother. He had seen a small metal box on the bottom of the car, on the outside just under the door. He pulled the little box off the car and stood up. He was excited.

"Look, Mum," he said. "I think Dad has saved Sherlock. I remember now that Dad put this box under the car. It stays on the car with a magnet. I think there are spare car keys in it." Max opened the box carefully. Inside it were the car keys! "Yippee," he shouted. "Good old Dad, he's saved us!"

Mrs Bradley looked as if she had seen a ghost.

"Why didn't he tell me about those spare keys," she said.

"He probably thought you'd think he was an idiot," said Max.

Max opened the car door with one of the keys and a very happy Sherlock jumped out and put his paws on Max's shoulders.

"I'm really sorry I did such a stupid thing, love," said Mrs Bradley. "It was dangerous to get so tired."

"Yep, we almost had a real hot dog for our picnic," said Max.

After a good snack and a break, Mrs Bradley drove north again for another couple of hours on the motorway. Max noticed that the countryside was starting to change. There were more hills on the left and right, and through the front window Max could see mountains.

Suddenly there was a sign that said: "Welcome to Scotland". Max took off his headphones.

"Wow, those mountains are really cool," he said.

Even Sherlock stood up and put his head out of the window to smell the Scottish air.

"Not long now," said Mrs Bradley. "We'll be in Edinburgh in about an hour, just in time for dinner."

The first thing Max saw as they got closer to the city was Edinburgh castle. It was lit up in a fantastic blue light and stood high on a rock.

"Amazing," said Max.

Mrs Bradley nodded. "The whole city is built on old volcanic rocks like that," she said.

They drove past the castle and five minutes later she stopped the car outside a big house.

"Here we are. This is where we're staying," said Mrs Bradley.

Max looked at his mother with surprise. "Aren't we staying in a hotel?" he asked.

"No, I couldn't find one where dogs are allowed to stay, or at least a big dog like Sherlock," said Mrs Bradley.

"So, who are we staying with?" asked Max.

"We are staying with somebody who knew your father when he was at university – Sir Charles Stewart."

"Oh, he's the guy who sends us a Christmas card every year?" asked Max.

"Yes, that's right," said Mrs Bradley.

"Why haven't I met him before?" asked Max.

"Well, you met him when you were very young, but of course you don't remember. He moved to Germany about ten years ago. His wife died a couple of years ago, and Charles came back to Scotland last year with his daughter, Tess. She lives here too so you'll meet her," said Mrs Bradley.

"He has a daughter? How old is she?" asked Max a bit worried. The last thing he wanted to do was to hang out with a stupid girl who was younger than him.

"Tess is older than you. She's almost 19, I think," said Mrs Bradley. "She's studying music at the university here."

"Cool," said Max. "Maybe she can show me the sights of Edinburgh while you're working."

"Yes, that's the plan," said Mrs Bradley, "then we can all do something together in the evenings."

Max didn't say anything – his thoughts were running in his head. He hadn't expected to meet a girl, or somebody who knew his father. He got out of the car with Sherlock and they both looked up at the big house. Maybe Scotland was going to be more interesting after all.

"Don't just stand there, Max, can you give me a hand with these bags?" asked Mrs Bradley as she opened the boot.

"Oh, sorry, Mum," said Max.

Mrs Bradley knocked on the front door of Sir Charles' house with a big door knocker that looked like a lion's head.

"Sir Charles is nice when you get to know him," whispered Mrs Bradley to Max as they waited for somebody to open the door, "but he's very Scottish."

"What do you mean?" asked Max. "What's 'very Scottish'?"

Mrs Bradley didn't have time to answer. The door suddenly opened and a tall man, who was smiling and wearing a kilt, stood in the doorway. It was Sir Charles. Max's eyes almost fell out of his head. He had never seen a man wear a kilt and sporran before. Maybe that's what his mum had meant by 'very Scottish'.

"Kate, it's good to see you again after so many years," he said.

"You, too, Charles," said Mrs Bradley.

As Sir Charles started to give Mrs Bradley a hug, Sherlock growled. Max was surprised because Sherlock was usually very friendly. Sherlock had never attacked anybody but Max grabbed Sherlock's collar in case Sherlock attacked Sir Charles.

"Quiet, Sherlock," said Max.

Sir Charles laughed. "Dinna fash yerself," he said.

"I'm sorry?" said Max, who had no idea what Sir Charles had just said.

"That's Gaelic for 'don't worry', said Sir Charles. Sherlock is just protecting your mother. He's probably never seen a man wearing a kilt before and thinks I'm a wild animal. Come in, both of you. Come in."

Max held onto Sherlock's collar so that he wouldn't run into the house, and then he and Mrs Bradley followed Sir Charles down the hall towards the living room.

"Mum, why is he wearing a kilt," whispered Max to his mother. "I thought Scotsmen don't wear them much any more."

"Well, maybe he's just wearing it because we are here and it's special," whispered Mrs Bradley, "although I read somewhere that more and more Scotsmen wear kilts these days and not just at special events."

When they all went into the living room Max couldn't believe his eyes – there were large deer heads on the walls, and above the fireplace there was a scary cat's head with big teeth. At first Max wasn't sure if it was dead or not. It looked like it was growling. But it was dead. Very dead.

Poor animal, Max thought as he looked at the cat's head. I wonder if Sir Charles killed all these animals. This is something out of a horror film.

Sir Charles came and stood next to Max.

"Well, what do you think of this collection?" asked Sir Charles.

"Er... well... er..."

Just as Max was thinking about what to say to Sir Charles, Sherlock started to push his nose into Sir Charles' sporran that was on the front of his kilt, hanging from his belt. Mrs Bradley looked shocked and Max pulled Sherlock away.

"Sorry about that," said Max.

Sir Charles patted his sporran and smiled.

"This sporran is made out of animal skin and fur – from that Scottish mountain cat that's over the fireplace, actually," said Sir Charles. "That's probably why Sherlock's interested in it.

"What is a sporran exactly?" asked Max.

"It's like a purse," said Sir Charles, "because a kilt doesn't have pockets."

"Oh, I see," said Max as he put his hands into his jeans' pockets and thought how terrible it was that a beautiful animal had been killed to be made into a purse.

"I'm sure you are both hungry so let's have dinner soon. My daughter Tess is out this evening so you won't meet her till the morning," said Sir Charles as he looked at Max. "I can't believe how much you've grown, Max. I think you were four or five years old the last time I saw you."

Max's face went red. He didn't know what to say and looked down at his feet. Why do adults always say such stupid and boring things? he thought.

"Er, that sounds wonderful," said Mrs Bradley. "Could Max give Sherlock some dinner in the kitchen?"

"Aye, of course," said Sir Charles, "just make yourselves at home."

"Thank you, Charles," said Mrs Bradley.

Max and Sherlock followed Sir Charles into the kitchen. This evening will be really boring with just Mum and this man who thinks it is fun to kill animals, Max thought.

Chapter 3 Big Issues in Edinburgh

When Max woke up the next morning, he wasn't quite sure where he was. All the walls in the room were dark wood, and a strict-looking Scotsman was looking at Max from a big painting on the wall opposite. There was a large sword and shield above Max's bed; Sherlock was asleep in a tartan dog bed on the floor. Then Max remembered: He was in Scotland. It felt like another country.

The house was quiet and Max looked at his watch. It was quite late so maybe everybody had gone out.

Suddenly there was a very loud noise – somebody in the house was starting to play the bagpipes. Sherlock woke up and started to howl like a wolf. Max put his fingers in his ears. He had never heard anything so horrible in his life! He quickly got dressed, ran out of the room and stood at the top of the stairs. Sherlock, who was still howling, followed him. A tall girl with short black hair stood at the bottom of the stairs. As soon as she saw Max, the girl stopped playing. Max took his fingers out of his ears and Sherlock stopped howling.

"Good morning, I'm Tess," she shouted up the stairs.

"I'm Max and this is Sherlock," Max shouted down to Tess.

"Aye, I know," shouted Tess back. "Are you both coming down for some breakfast or do you want to stay up there all day?"

"Breakfast is a great idea," said Max.

As Max started to go down the stairs Sherlock pushed past him and ran down to Tess wagging his tail. She put the bagpipes on a chair next to her and gave Sherlock a pat on his head. Sherlock licked her hand.

"Hello Sherlock," said Tess. "It's nice to meet you."

"He likes you," said Max as he stood next to Tess. "Er... do you usually play the bagpipes first thing in the morning for your guests? Is it a Scottish thing?"

Tess smiled at Max.

"No, not really, I just thought a wee bit of bagpipes would wake up the Sassenach," she said. Who could sleep through that noise? Max thought to himself. Then he asked:

"Where is everybody?"

"Your mum has already gone to take photos of the festival and my father has gone to a meeting or something. If you like, I could show you and your bonnie doggie some of the sights of the city."

"Sounds good," said Max.

About an hour later, Tess and Max were walking up a steep hill called Calton Hill. Sherlock was running in front of them.

"What did you call me earlier?" panted Max. "A sassen-something?"

"Ah, I called you a Sassenach. That's Gaelic for 'Englishman'. It's not a bad word or anything," smiled Tess. "Now, what do you think of the view?"

"Wow, that's amazing," said Max as they stood at the top of Calton Hill. Even Sherlock seemed to like it. He stood between Max and Tess and wagged his tail.

"We call Edinburgh 'Auld Reekie' which is Gaelic for 'Old Smokey'. In the old days, people had coal and wood fires so there was a lot of smoke in the air," said Tess.

"Like London. We call it the Big Smoke. What's that building west of the castle?"

"That's Holyroodhouse Palace, home of the Scottish kings and queens since the 16th century," explained Tess. "Behind the palace is Holyrood Park and those rocks over there are called the Salisbury Crags. If you like rock climbing and abseiling, we could go there tomorrow,"

"Er, rock climbing isn't really my thing," said Max. He was still a bit out of breath from the steep walk up the hill.

"Never mind, come on, Sassenach, there's more to see."

The city was full of tourists who had come to enjoy the Edinburgh festival with music, theatre and dance. Tess took Max and Sherlock through streets where there was a lot of street entertainment and live music, which was also a part of the festival. They stopped to watch a street artist who was wearing gold clothes and a gold hat. Even his hair and skin were gold. He was like a statue and only moved when somebody put some money into the box.

"Look at that guy," said Max to Tess. "How can he stand like that for so long? That's amazing."

Just then, Sherlock stood next to the 'statue', lifted his back leg and quickly peed on the gold shoes. Max expected the 'statue' to start shouting at Sherlock, but nothing happened. The 'statue' didn't move.

"Now that *is* amazing," laughed Tess. "I think we should put some money in his box for that, don't you?"

"Yeah," said Max, "and I think we should go somewhere else or Sherlock might get more ideas."

They walked along Candlemaker Row and Tess showed Max and Sherlock a statue of a little Highland terrier dog called Greyfriars Bobby.

"When this wee dog's master died, the sad dog stayed by his master's grave every day," explained Tess.

"Sherlock will always stay by me too, won't you," said Max as he gave Sherlock a pat on his head.

"Sherlock seems to do his own thing," laughed Tess.

When they got to the bottom of Calton Hill they walked along Princes Street and then went into Princes Street Gardens. Max put Sherlock on his lead.

"It's hard to believe that these beautiful gardens were once the Nor' Loch – a lake that all the sewage of the Old Town went into," explained Tess.

"Yuck," said Max.

"Let's go through that gate towards the castle," said Tess. "We can't go in the castle because dogs aren't allowed in. It's an interesting place to visit because you can see the oldest crown jewels in Europe."

"Are there cannons in the castle?" asked Max.

"Oh yes, there's a very big one called Mons Meg," said Tess. "It was used in a big battle between the English and the Scots, er... I'm not sure when, about 500 years ago, I think."

"Who won?" asked Max.

"You Sassenachs won, but don't let it go to your head," smiled Tess.

Just then she looked at her watch.

"Now, make sure you've got Sherlock under control," she said, "because any minute now there's going to be a big..."

Tess didn't get a chance to finish what she was saying because suddenly there was a very loud bang!

"What was that?" asked Max, looking worried. He pulled Sherlock close to him. "That sounded like an explosion. Was it a bomb?"

"That was a cannon," she explained. "You can hear it every day at 1pm. It goes back to the old days when most people didn't have clocks or watches. When they heard the cannon, they knew it was 1 o'clock. Today it's just an old tradition."

"Phew, that's scary if you don't know it's going to happen," said Max.

"Sherlock doesn't look too scared or worried," said Tess. "That's amazing. Most dogs run away if they hear a loud bang like that. Come on, it's time for lunch."

A few minutes later, they were sitting at a table outside Nicolson's Cafe. Sherlock sat on the ground next to Max with his lead around the leg of Max's chair.

"I thought you might like to come to this cafe," said Tess. "It's where J.K. Rowling wrote the first Harry Potter book because she was too poor to buy coal to keep her flat warm."

"Wow," said Max.

"They do a really good haggis burger here," said Tess.

"What's haggis?" asked Max.

"It's a kind of large sausage and very traditional," said Tess.

"That sounds good. I'll try it," said Max.

Tess went inside the cafe to order their food and about 15 minutes later the waiter brought two haggis burgers to the table. He also brought a big bowl of water for Sherlock.

"This haggis stuff is really good," said Max as he tried some. "I wonder if Sherlock will like it."

Max took a bit of haggis and gave it to Sherlock, who sniffed it and then ate it.

Just then a girl about Max's age walked towards their table. She had a dog with her and had a bag full of magazines on her shoulder. As soon as Sherlock saw the girl's dog, he started to pull on his lead. When the girl had got to the table, the two dogs started to sniff each other.

"Oh, I think they like each other," said Max to the girl. "Your dog is very sweet. What's her name?"

"Maggie," said the girl. "Your dog is very friendly too. What's his name?"

"Sherlock," answered Max.

"Oh, like Sherlock Holmes," said the girl.

Max smiled.

"Actually I sometimes call him Sherlock Bones, because he loves those dog biscuits that look like bones."

"Maggie likes those too," said the girl. "Sherlock is an Old English sheepdog, isn't he?" But he's got a tail – I've never seen one with a tail. It's a big tail, too."

"You don't often see this kind of dog with a tail because the owner usually cuts off the tail when the dog is born," said Max.

"That is so cruel!" said the girl. "Why do they do that?"

"Owners think that these dogs look better without tails. They also think that it's safer for the dog if it doesn't have one – the dog might get its tail caught in something while it's working with sheep."

"That's interesting," said Tess. "I never knew that."

"Yeah, but more and more countries don't allow the tails to be cut off – it's not legal any more," explained Max.

sue

"Well, that's good," said the girl, "because how would Sherlock show us he's happy if he didn't have a tail to wag?"

They all looked at Sherlock. He was wagging his tail very fast, almost hitting poor Maggie in her face with it.

"Would you like to buy one of these magazines?" asked the girl. "I keep half the money and the rest goes to other homeless people like me."

Max looked surprised and didn't know what to say. He had had no idea that the girl was homeless, or maybe a runaway.

"It must be very hard for you to be homeless and have a dog too," said Tess.

"Yeah, how can you look after her?" asked Max. "It's expensive to have a dog. My mum is always grumbling about how much money she spends on Sherlock."

"Maggie is my only friend," said the girl. "People think that street dogs aren't looked after, but my dog is healthier than most sitting-room dogs. I'd be in prison if I didn't have Maggie. I don't spend my money on alcohol – I buy food for her instead. She's the only reason why I wake up in the morning. I only stay in homeless shelters where my dog is allowed to stay. If my dog can't go in, I sleep on the street."

"But isn't it dangerous on the street?" asked Tess.

"Yeah, sometimes it is, but dogs are better than people. Maggie protects me on the street. She barks to warn me if there's danger," said the girl.

Max got some money out of his pocket and gave it to the girl.

"Here you are," he said. "I'll buy one of your magazines."

"Thank you so much," said the girl as she gave one to Max. "Is it OK if I give Sherlock a biscuit?"

"Oh, yes, he would love that," said Max.

The girl reached into her bag and took out a little plastic bag that was filled with dog biscuits that looked like bones.

"Here you are, Sherlock," she said, "I've got one of your favourite biscuits."

Sherlock sat and carefully took the biscuit from the girl's hand. Then the girl gave a biscuit to Maggie.

"Goodbye Sherlock Bones," said the girl, "it was nice to meet you," she said as she patted Sherlock on his head. "Nice to meet you, too," she said to Max and Tess.

"Take care," said Max and Tess together.

As the girl walked down the street with her dog, Sherlock pulled on his lead – he wanted to follow the girl's dog.

"Lie down Sherlock," said Max. "You can't go with them."

Sherlock lay on the ground next to Max's chair and put his head on his large paws. He looked sad.

"That was nice of you to buy one of her magazines," said Tess to Max.

"Well, she needs the money, and she was right – I don't know what I would do without Sherlock," said Max as he patted Sherlock on his head. "He's my best friend."

Sherlock licked Max's hand.

The next day Max and Tess went to visit Edinburgh castle and the Museum of Scotland. Mrs Bradley had finished her work so she looked after Sherlock. In the afternoon they sat in the sitting room with Sir Charles and chatted.

"Are you having a good time in Edinburgh, Max?" asked Sir Charles.

"Yes I am. The city is very interesting. I'd like to see more of Scotland."

"That's good to hear. Actually, I've got an idea. Would you all like to go to my cottage in Crathie for two days? It's about three hours drive. Sherlock will like it – he'll be in the middle of nature and he'll have lots of deer to chase. What do you think, Kate? You don't have to run back to London, do you?" asked Sir Charles as he looked at Mrs Bradley.

"That's very nice of you, Charles. Is that OK with you, Max?" asked Mrs Bradley.

"Great! Er... can Tess come with us?" asked Max.

Tess smiled. "Dinna fash yersel Sassenach. Crathie is my favourite place in the world," she said.

"Good," said Sir Charles. "Shall we go in my car? It's got a central lock system so there's no chance of Sherlock locking himself inside!"

"That's probably a good idea," said Max.

They all laughed and looked at Sherlock, who was wagging his tail.

Chapter 4 Dark clouds over Loch Muick

The next morning, after breakfast, they left Edinburgh very early. Max sat in the front with Sir Charles, and Tess and Mrs Bradley sat in the back with Sherlock. They drove along small roads, past big fields, towards the mountains. Sometimes there was a small cottage in a valley but they never saw any people, only sheep. Max felt like he was the only human on earth. Even Sherlock was interested in the countryside and looked out of the window. He probably thought that he was the only dog on earth!

"Only five million people live in Scotland," said Sir Charles as if he was reading Max's thoughts.

"England's got a lot more people, about 50 million, I think," said Max.

"Yes, that sounds about right but it's only twice as big as Scotland," said Sir Charles.

Max smiled at Sir Charles and then looked out of the window. He wondered if Sir Charles had taught his father at university. I'll ask Mum later, he thought.

Soon the road had lots of hills and bends. The car went up and down – it was a bit like a roller coaster. Usually roller coasters are fun, but not if you ride on them for two hours! Max felt a bit sick. He wanted to throw up.

Just then there was a voice from the back of the car.

"Oh, dear, Sherlock's nose is very hot and he doesn't look very comfortable," said Mrs Bradley. "He looks like he's feeling a bit sick or something."

"Yes, he does." said Tess. "Can we stop for a moment, Dad?"

Max turned round and looked at Sherlock, who was now between Tess and his mum. Sherlock was trying to stand up as if he wanted to get out of the car. Max wasn't surprised that Sherlock was feeling how Max felt – a bit green!

"OK," said Sir Charles. "I can't stop here; it's too dangerous because there are too many bends and there isn't anywhere to park. When the road gets a bit straighter and there's a place to park, I'll stop. OK?"

"Thanks, Charles," said Mrs Bradley.

"Yes, thanks," said Max to Sir Charles.

Max turned around again to look at Sherlock in the back of the car. Sherlock looked at Mrs Bradley, then at Tess, and then at Mrs Bradley again. Then he opened his mouth and threw up all over Mrs Bradley's jeans!

"Oh, Sherlock!" cried Max. "Sorry, Mum..."

"Oh dear, well, it's not his fault," said Mrs Bradley.

Tess gave Mrs Bradley a big box of tissues so that she could clean her jeans a bit.

Max looked at his mother and couldn't believe that she wasn't angry that Sherlock had ruined her jeans. It was a good thing, too, that Sherlock hadn't thrown up on Tess. That would have been worse! he thought.

The last part of the journey to Sir Charles' country house went OK. There weren't so many curves, and Sherlock didn't throw up again.

"We're almost there now," said Sir Charles.

Just then he drove very slowly past two big gates.

"Behind those gates is Balmoral Castle. It's the Queen's Scottish home. It's very near my house so we're neighbours," laughed Sir Charles.

"Is the Queen here now?" asked Max.

"Yes, she is," answered Sir Charles.

Max' mouth fell open. I must send a text to Zack later. He won't believe me! he thought.

"The Queen always comes here at this time of year to hunt deer and grouse," said Sir Charles.

"How can she kill animals if she likes nature so much?" asked Max.

"That's a good question. The royal family have always hunted so I think it's in their blood," said Sir Charles.

"The Queen is also here because of the Highland Games," said Tess from the back of the car.

"Yes, that's right," said Sir Charles. "The village of Braemar is near here and it has its own Highland Games, which is called the Braemar Gathering. The Queen and her family come every year to watch and give the prizes."

"Maybe I can enter the bagpipe competition. I brought my bagpipes with me!" said Tess.

"But I didn't bring my earplugs!" cried Max.

Just then Sherlock started to howl.

"You see? Sherlock hates bagpipes, too," laughed Max.

"Don't be so smart, Sassenach," smiled Tess, "but don't worry, I didn't really bring them. I was just joking."

"Do they have sheepdog competitions," asked Max, "where sheepdogs try to put sheep into different pens? Sherlock would like that."

"Yes, he might learn something," laughed Tess. "He's such a numptie."

"What's a numptie?" asked Max.

"It's a nice Gaelic name for an idiot," said Tess.

Max looked upset.

"He's not an idiot, Tess. He's more intelligent than you think. He's just young," said Max.

"Now, you're being a numptie," said Tess.

"Oh, you're joking again," smiled Max. "Now I get it."

When they arrived at Sir Charles' cottage there was a land rover parked outside.

"Ah, good, I see that Mr McDonald is here," said Sir Charles. "He lives down the road and looks after the cottage when I'm in Edinburgh."

"Oh, what a lovely cottage," said Mrs Bradley as she got out of the car.

"Thank you. I feel that I can really relax here, away from the mad city life."

Max nodded. He wished that he could live somewhere like this, in the countryside with mountains all around, and not in their flat in London. He had always thought that he liked living in a big city – there was always something to see or do – but now that he was in the middle of the Scottish Highlands, he really liked the quietness and beauty of nature.

As soon as everybody got out of the car, a friendly white Highland terrier ran up to them.

"This is Murdo," said Sir Charles. "He belongs to Mr McDonald."

"He's a sweet dog," said Max to his mother as they watched Murdo and Sherlock playing together.

"Yes, he is," said Mrs Bradley. "And he's small, too."

Max gave his mother an angry look. He knew that she had always wanted a small dog and that Sherlock was too big.

Just then a man in his sixties came towards Sir Charles.

"Ah, here's Mr McDonald," said Sir Charles. "He can't hear very well, so you have to speak loudly to him."

"Hello, Sir Charles, good to see you," said Mr McDonald as he shook Sir Charles' hand.

"Did you have a good journey?"

"Yes, thank you, but I don't think all of my guests liked the bends in the mountain road," said Sir Charles as he looked at Sherlock who was still playing with Murdo.

"I'll make some tea and bring it out to you all in the garden," said Mr McDonald.

"That's very nice of you," said Sir Charles. "Kate, Max, come with me. I'll show you to your rooms first."

About 30 minutes later, Max and Mrs Bradley joined Tess and Sir Charles in the garden. Then Mr McDonald came and gave everybody a cup of tea and some biscuits.

"Thank you, Mr McDonald," said Sir Charles. "We'll all feel much better after a cup of your strong tea."

"Um, Tess, do you think I can get on the internet here?" asked Max. "I've brought my laptop with me."

"Do you need to use the phone line?" asked Tess.

"Well, I've got a USB modem, but it might not work if the mountains block the satellite signal."

"I've got one of those, too," said Tess. "Mine works OK here."

"Great, I'll give it a try," said Max.

Tess sat with her father and Mrs Bradley. Max opened his laptop and after a few minutes he was online. He looked over at Tess, who was listening to Mrs Bradley as she was talking to Sir Charles about London. Just then Tess looked over at Max and mouthed to him: "Does it work?"

Max smiled and nodded to her – in fact he was already chatting to Zack online:

Zack: How's Edinburgh?
Max: It was Gr8. We are up in Aberdeenshire now
Zack: Where?
Max: Crathie. Guess who our neighbour is
Zack: J.K. Rowling?
Max: Queen!
Zack: Cool. Take a plastic bag if she invites you and Sherl to tea ;-))
Max: Ha ha

Sir Charles looked at his watch and stood up. Sherlock and Murdo stopped playing and came over to Sir Charles as if they expected something.

"Who's ready for a picnic in Glenn Muick and then a short walk?" he asked. "Mr McDonald has prepared the picnic so we could leave in about 30 minutes."

"That sounds wonderful to me," said Mrs Bradley, "how about you, Max?"

"Fine with me," said Max as he turned off his laptop.

"How short, Dad?" asked Tess. "There's a Sassenach here who isn't very sporty."

"I'm not good at climbing, that's all," grumbled Max, "I walk with Sherlock all the time."

"Well, the walk around Loch Muick is about nine miles," said Sir Charles. "Murdo and Sherlock will love it. It will take us about three hours."

Max's mouth fell open. If Sir Charles thought nine miles was a short walk, what did he think a long walk was?

"Come on Max, you can do it," smiled Tess.

"Yes, of course you can." said Sir Charles. "If you're anything like your father, you like walking. We went on long hikes together when we were at university."

"I didn't know that about Dad," said Max, who was amazed to hear something new about his father. "Were you a professor? Did you teach my dad?"

"Oh no," said Sir Charles smiling, "I was a student too, in the same year as your dad. We became friends because we both belonged to the hiking group. I've got some photos of him on one of those hikes. I can show them to you when we come back if you like."

"That would be great, thanks. That is, if Tess thinks I'll survive the walk," said Max. He was proud that he had made a joke about himself. Tess smiled at him.

About three hours later, they were all walking along the side of Loch Muick. Murdo, the Highland terrier, walked between Sir Charles and Mrs Bradley. Tess and Max walked behind them. Sherlock ran in front of them all, and then ran back to them, then behind and then in front again as if they were sheep. The group was too slow for him. He wanted them to walk faster.

"We might see some red deer on our walk if we are lucky," Tess told Max. "They are so beautiful when you see them in the wood."

"Well, I hope your father won't kill them," said Max. "I've never seen so many dead animals in somebody's living room before."

"Oh, you mean in the house in Edinburgh. Dad didn't kill those," said Tess. "He actually doesn't like hunting."

"So who killed all those animals?" asked Max, who felt a bit stupid that he had blamed Sir Charles.

"The house belonged to my grandfather and he liked to hunt animals," said Tess. "Balmoral Castle is very near here and this whole area belongs to the Queen, so my grandfather did a lot of hunting around here."

"I wonder how many dead animal heads the Queen has got on her walls," said Max.

"We'll never find out," said Tess. "Hmmm, look at those dark clouds over Lochnager. It looks like there'll be a storm or something."

"Lochnager?" said Max. "I just see a mountain. Is that what you mean? Is that what you call mountains here in Scotland – a Lochnager?"

"No," laughed Tess. "We call mountains Munros. Well, if they are more than about 900 metres high, we call them Munros. Lochnager is the name of that Munro over there. It's about 1000 metres high. We could climb it tomorrow if you like."

"Ha, ha," said Max, "but 1000 metres isn't very high."

"No, it isn't, but these Munros can be dangerous. A jet plane crashed on one here about 60 years ago. Parts of the plane are still up there. A lot of rock climbers, and even hikers, have serious accidents on Munros in this area."

"That's another good reason not to do rock climbing," joked Max.

After about three miles, the trail went through woods and became steeper. The walk was more difficult. Everybody stopped talking. It was very quiet and kind of scary. They could just hear the wind. Just then, there was a different sound. Something very big moved in the trees. Murdo growled but Sherlock started to bark and wag his tail. He was very excited and ran around with his nose on the ground.

"It's probably just a large red deer," said Sir Charles. "Sherlock can smell it."

Then suddenly, without any warning, Sherlock ran into the woods as fast as a rocket.

"Sherlock, come back!" called Max.

Everybody waited, but Sherlock didn't come back. Max called again, and again. There was nothing but silence.

Sherlock was gone!

"I don't believe it. He's run off. He's never done that before," said Max.

"Murdo didn't run off. You stayed here to protect us, didn't you?" said Mrs Bradley as she patted Murdo on his head.

Max gave his mother an angry look. Didn't she even care that Sherlock had run off? And how could a little dog like Murdo protect anybody?

"We have to go after him," he said loudly.

"I don't think we'll be able to catch him now," said Sir Charles. "It's probably best if we keep calling him and wait here."

"I've got an idea, Dad," said Tess. Why don't Max and I go after Sherlock and you two stay here with Murdo? We've got mobile phones in case something happens."

"Is that OK with you, Kate?" asked Sir Charles.

Mrs Bradley nodded. "But let's call in about an hour, or we'll lose you too. And be careful," she said with a worried voice.

Max and Tess walked and ran through the woods together as fast as they could, calling Sherlock's name. There was no sign of him. About 20 minutes later, Max stopped.

"I can't run any more. Let's rest a minute," he panted.

"OK," said Tess. Suddenly she saw something on the ground. "What's that over there?" she said.

They both walked over to look at what she had seen.

"Oh no," cried Max. "It's Sherlock's collar. If somebody finds him, they won't know who to call."

"I think we'd better tell Dad. Sherlock could be miles away by now," said Tess as she took her mobile out of her pocket.

Max sat on the ground with Sherlock's collar in his hands. "Yeah, I guess so," he said.

"Hi Dad, it's me. We're coming back," Tess said. "It doesn't look very good. We've found Sherlock's collar, but no Sherlock!"

When Max and Tess got back to Sir Charles and Mrs Bradley, they showed them Sherlock's dog collar.

"Let's go back to the house and get the land rovers," said Sir Charles. "They'll be easier to drive on and off the roads. You can drive one Tess, and take Max with you. I'll drive Mr McDonald's. Kate, maybe you should stay at the cottage in case Sherlock finds his way there."

"OK, that sounds like a good plan," said Tess.

Mrs Bradley nodded.

Sir Charles looked at the dark clouds in the sky. "There's a storm coming, so let's go," he said.

Chapter 5 The royal hunt

Sherlock ran as fast as a rocket and tried to catch the large red deer, but it could run faster so it soon disappeared. The tired and thirsty dog stopped by the river for a drink of fresh cold water. The side of the river was quite high. As Sherlock tried to reach the water, he fell into it with a big splash! When he found a place where he could get out, he climbed up and shook himself dry. Then he walked, and walked. After about 30 minutes Sherlock stopped and listened. It was very quiet. He sniffed the air. He couldn't smell any deer, and he couldn't smell Max, so he lay down on the ground under a tree and went to sleep as it started to rain...

About three miles away, Tess was driving her father's land rover and Max was sitting beside her. He was looking out of the window and was very worried.

"Oh, no, now it's raining, and Sherlock hates the rain," he said. "He doesn't even like to go for walks much when it's raining."

Tess turned on the windscreen wipers. "Maybe he's found somewhere dry," she said, "you know, like under a tree or something."

Tess drove along the road slowly so that she and Max could look for Sherlock.

After a while, Max's mobile beeped.

"It's from my friend Zack," said Max as he read Zack's message:

How r u?

"I have to tell him what's happened," said Max to Tess.

He quickly sent an answer to Zack:

Not gd. Sherl ran away. We r looking 4 him. We have found his collar...

Max's phone beeped again:

That's v bad news! Hope u find him. Let's chat L8er. Maybe I can help...

Max sent another text:

OK mate. Thx

A few minutes later Tess's mobile rang. She parked the land rover at the side of the road and answered it.

"Hi Dad, what's up?" she asked.

Max looked at Tess and hoped that her father would have some good news, but Tess was looking at Max and shaking her head.

"OK," said Tess to her father. "That's a good idea. Talk soon. Bye."

"What did he say?" asked Max.

"He's still driving around with your mum, but there's a farm near here that belongs to a friend of his. He thinks we should look for Sherlock there," said Tess. "He'll tell the farmer that we're coming."

"Yeah, he might not be anywhere near the roads," said Max, "he might be running over the fields or something."

She turned left and drove the land rover into a small road and then stopped in front of a gate. Max got out and opened it so that Tess could drive through. Then he closed it again.

"It's raining really hard now," he said as he climbed into the land rover, "poor Sherlock."

"Did you get Sherlock when he was a puppy?" asked Tess.

"Yep," said Max. "My dad gave him to me about four years ago. He travelled a lot because of his work and thought

Mum and I needed a dog to protect us when he wasn't at home. Mum didn't like the idea but she agreed in the end. Sherlock gets on her nerves a bit."

They drove around the large farm for about an hour, across fields where they could, but there was still no sign of Sherlock.

"It's getting late, and dark because of this horrible weather," said Tess. "I think we should go back to the house; Dad's probably already there. We'll look for Sherlock first thing in the morning. With a bit of luck he might be in a nice warm cottage somewhere for the night."

"OK, I hope you're right," said Max. He could feel tears coming to his eyes and looked out of the window – he didn't want Tess to see that he was crying.

Early next morning, Sherlock woke up and looked around for something to eat. There was nothing, not even an old haggis sandwich or a packet of crisps. Suddenly he heard a loud gunshot and a bird fell onto the ground in front of him – it was dead! Sherlock sniffed the bird; it smelled good enough to eat and he was very hungry but he had no idea how to eat it.

Just then Sherlock heard two voices:

"Good shot, Ma'am!"

"Thank you. Send the dog to find it and bring it."

A minute later, a black Labrador appeared and ran towards Sherlock and the dead bird. The Labrador growled at Sherlock. Sherlock looked at the Labrador and wagged his tail, but the Labrador was too busy to chat or play – he was the Queen's dog and had an important job to do. He picked up the bird carefully with his mouth and then ran off. Sherlock followed him.

The Labrador ran towards a small group of people and then dropped the bird at the feet of a woman who was carrying a gun under her arm and wearing green wellies. It was the Queen! A tall young man stood beside her – it was her grandson Prince William. The Labrador sat in front of the Queen and Sherlock sat beside the Labrador. Both dogs were wagging their tails and looking at the Queen.

"Oh, look at that, Grandma," laughed Prince William, "the gamekeeper's dog has found a very strange bird – it's an English sheepdog kind of bird. And it's a very dirty and wet one, too."

Sherlock wagged his tail a bit faster and the Queen frowned.

"He looks like he's been out here all night," said the Queen. "He's lost and his owner is probably very sad and is trying to find him."

"What are we going to do with him, Grandma?" asked Prince William.

"Is he wearing a collar?" the Queen asked her gamekeeper, who was standing next to Prince William

The gamekeeper gave his gun to his assistant and felt Sherlock's neck with his hands.

"No Ma'am," he said.

"Well, we can't leave him here – he might get shot! Take him back to the castle and give him a good breakfast," said the Queen. "Then take him to the vet in Braemar. The dog might have a microchip and the vet will be able to read it and contact the owner."

"Yes, Ma'am," said the gamekeeper. "Come on, doggie, let's give you some breakfast."

"Breakfast" was one of Sherlock's favourite words so he wagged his tail really fast and followed the gamekeeper to

his land rover. The black Labrador went with the Queen and Prince William, who wanted to see if they could shoot another bird or two before breakfast.

At Sir Charles' cottage, Max had got up very early because he couldn't sleep. He was too worried about Sherlock. He quietly went downstairs with his laptop, sat at the large table in the kitchen and turned on his computer to check his e-mails. There was one from Zack:

Hi Max
Any news about Sherlock? What happened? How did he get lost? He's an intelligent dog so probably he'll find his way back to you, or maybe somebody found him and will take him to a dog rescue centre.
It might be an idea to make posters with a picture of him and put them in the local shops.
Keep me posted.
Zack

That's a really good idea, thought Max, I can make a poster on my laptop while everybody is still asleep. He quickly wrote back to Zack:

Hi Zack
Thanks for your e-mail – it's really good to hear from you.
No news yet...
We went for a long walk yesterday and Sherlock smelled a deer or something and ran after it. He didn't come back when I called him.
We all drove around to look for him until quite late.
I'm really worried that somebody has found him and will keep him because he isn't wearing his collar and they can't contact me –

we found his collar yesterday in the place where he ran away.
I hope that if somebody found him, they won't sell him. Remember what you told me about dog thieves?
He has a microchip with my contact information on it, so maybe somebody will take him to a rescue centre or the police.
I'll make a poster now – great idea, thanks. I hope the people we're staying with have a printer.
I'll let you know if there's any news... Let's hope it will be good news.
Max

About two hours later, Tess came downstairs and went into the kitchen where Max was still sitting.

"You're up early," she said as she put some water in a kettle to make a cup of tea.

"Yeah, I couldn't sleep," said Max. "Look I've made a 'lost' poster. What do you think of it? Is it OK?"

"It's really good," said Tess as she looked at the screen on Max's laptop. "That's a really cool photo of Sherlock, and you can see his tail, which is important."

"Thanks, my dad took it," said Max. "Is there a printer here?"

"Yep, there's one in my father's room," said Tess. "We'll have to wait until he gets up."

"Great," said Max, "then we can print out some copies and put them in shops or something."

"Aye, and we can make some copies in Braemar if we need more," said Tess.

Max looked at his watch.

"Why are Mum and your dad still asleep?" he said. "We're wasting time sitting around here."

"Dad usually gets up very early so he'll probably be down soon," said Tess.

"It's sad you didn't bring your bagpipes," said Max.

"Why?" asked Tess, who looked very surprised.

"Well, you could have played them and woken everybody up," smiled Max.

Tess smiled back at him.

"You're getting quite good at making jokes," she said. "Would you like some tea and toast?"

"OK," said Max.

He closed his laptop and pushed it to the other side of the table. Tess put two cups of tea and two plates of hot buttered toast on the table and then sat next to him. They ate and drank without saying anything.

I don't know how I would get through all this without Tess, Max thought.

About 15 minutes later Sir Charles came downstairs and joined Max and Tess in the kitchen.

"That toast smells good," he said.

"Dad, Max has made a 'lost' poster with Sherlock's picture on it. Could he use your printer to print out some copies?" asked Tess.

"Of course," said Sir Charles. "Show Max where it is."

"Thanks," said Max as he followed Tess upstairs.

When Max and Tess had finished printing they went downstairs into the kitchen. Mrs Bradley was sitting at the kitchen table with Sir Charles.

"Hi Mum," said Max.

"Did you get some sleep, love?" asked Mrs Bradley.

"Not much, but I made these posters. I think they came out really well," said Max as he gave one to his mother.

"Oh," said Mrs Bradley as she looked at the poster.

"What's the matter with it?" asked Max.

"Nothing, but that's a photo that your dad took, isn't it?" asked Mrs Bradley. "I've taken so many great photos of Sherlock. Why didn't you use one of mine?"

"I like this one... er... because it shows his tail really well," said Max.

He took the poster out of his mother's hand.

"I suppose it does," said Mrs Bradley.

She looked at her teacup.

I don't know why she's so upset, thought Max angrily. Sherlock is missing and she's only thinking about her photos.

Sir Charles looked at Max and Mrs Bradley and then at his watch.

"Well, let's make a plan for the day and the best way to find Sherlock," he said. "I think Kate and I should drive to more farms around here and tell the farmers about Sherlock. We'll take some of your posters with us, Max."

Max nodded.

"Great "said Tess. "Max and I will go to Braemar and put some posters in the shops there, and the post office. There'll be a lot of people going there today because it's the last day of the Games and they will want to see the Queen."

"What about Balmoral Castle?" asked Max. "Let's look around there, too."

"Hmmm, the castle is closed at the moment because the Queen is staying there," said Sir Charles.

"But it's a good idea to drive around and look in people's cars as they drive past. Maybe somebody will pick up Sherlock," said Mrs Bradley.

"You mean, steal him," said Max angrily, "to sell him for drugs."

"Don't be silly, Max," said Mrs Bradley. "He can't be too far from here. I know you're upset. So am I. But let's have breakfast and then we'll go and find him."

Max's face suddenly went red. He was angry.

"How can I eat breakfast when Sherlock is missing?" he shouted. "You're not upset. You're probably happy that he's gone. You're jealous of him because Dad gave him to me."

Mrs Bradley's eyes filled up with tears. "Max, that's not true," she cried.

"Sherlock could be dead or hurt, or locked in a dark place with no food and you just want to eat stupid breakfast!" shouted Max.

He ran out of the kitchen and banged the door shut.

At Balmoral Castle it was breakfast time, too. Sherlock was playing in a garden with two other dogs that belonged to the Queen's gamekeeper. There was a big bowl of fresh, cold water under a tree and the dogs took it in turns to have long drinks. As soon as the gamekeeper came into the garden, the three dogs stopped playing and ran up to him because he was carrying three big bowls of dog food.

"Sit!" said the gamekeeper, "and wait!"

The three dogs all sat, but as the gamekeeper put the bowls on the ground, Sherlock stood up and ran to one of the bowls and started to eat.

"Hey, you are a hungry doggie," the gamekeeper said to Sherlock. "OK, you two, you can eat now," he told the others.

The gamekeeper's dogs stood up and went to their bowls. Sherlock had already eaten his food and was now trying to eat the bowl. The gamekeeper gave Sherlock a bit more food and then let him play with the other two dogs. About an hour later he came back to the garden.

"I wish we could keep you loon. You're a very nice doggie, but Her Majesty has asked me to take you to Braemar," he said.

The gamekeeper took a collar out of his pocket.

"You'll have to wear this until we get to the vet," the gamekeeper explained as he put the collar around Sherlock's neck.

Sherlock wagged his tail and followed the gamekeeper to his land rover. The gamekeeper opened the back door and Sherlock jumped in.

Tess and Max were driving towards Balmoral Castle. Tess looked at Max. She knew he was still angry.

"You can tell me to mind my own business, but do you want to tell me what happened to your dad?" she asked.

"It's OK," he said. "Dad died in a car accident. Mum needed to use Dad's car so a colleague from work drove him to the office. Their car was hit by another car that was going too fast on the motorway. Dad died in hospital three days later. His colleague died in the car."

Max could feel the tears coming to his eyes but it felt good to talk to somebody about his dad. Tess didn't say anything, but she nodded her head very slowly and looked very sad.

"Why didn't she go by train or something on that day?" Max asked Tess. "Why did she need to use my dad's car? She always thinks about herself."

Max looked out of the window and wiped a tear from his cheek.

"Max, it's probably hard for her too," said Tess quietly. "She probably blames herself too, but the accident wasn't her fault. It just happened."

Max didn't say anything at first but after a moment or two he said, "I suppose so."

Just then, as Tess drove past Balmoral Castle, the large gates of the castle were slowly opening and a royal land rover was waiting to drive out.

"Did you see that land rover?" asked Tess. "It had a little flag on the front of it. I wonder if the Queen was driving. I couldn't quite see..."

"Yeah, yeah, and maybe she found Sherlock and he's in the back," said Max.

"Ha, ha," said Tess, smiling. "Now, that would be funny."

Max looked out of the window again, but this time he was smiling a bit, too.

Chapter 6 The Games

The Queen's gamekeeper drove through the gates of Balmoral Castle and then towards the village of Braemar. Soon he was driving behind Max and Tess, who were going quite slowly.

"Those people must be toonsers," said the gamekeeper out loud as he passed them. "They're driving as slow as a snail and looking at the sights so they can't be from around here."

Sherlock opened one eye as the gamekeeper spoke, but then he closed it again. He just wanted to sleep after his big breakfast.

About half an hour later, the gamekeeper and Sherlock arrived in Braemar. The village was full of people – tourists, photographers and news reporters from the BBC – who were all there to see the last day of the Highland Games and to see the Queen. The Highland dancing competition was just finishing in a field and the audience clapped and cheered as the Queen gave the prize to the young girl who had won. Prince William, who was standing next to his grandmother, smiled at the girl and her face went very red. As she left, the Queen and Prince William sat down. The Queen took her glasses out of her handbag and put them on to read the programme.

The gamekeeper parked outside the vet's house in the high street and got out. He walked around to the back of the land rover and opened the back door. Sherlock stood up.

"Come on doggie," said the gamekeeper. "Let's go and see the vet and find your owner."

Sherlock jumped out and the gamekeeper grabbed him by the collar. When they got to the front door of the vet's house, the door opened and a young boy came out. He was carrying a puppy in his arms.

"Oh, that's a sweet young pup," said the gamekeeper to the boy.

The gamekeeper took his hand from Sherlock's collar so he could pat the puppy. Suddenly Sherlock knew where he was – he could smell the vet's room and the other animals. While the gamekeeper was patting the boy's puppy, Sherlock turned around and ran down the road before the gamekeeper could stop him.

"Come back, doggie," shouted the gamekeeper after Sherlock. "I'm trying to help you."

But Sherlock wasn't listening. He was running as fast as he could. The last person he wanted to see was a vet!

A few moments later Max and Tess arrived in Braemar. Tess drove along the high street and saw the royal land rover, which was parked outside a house.

"Is that the land rover that passed us on the road?" said Tess.

"Maybe. Everybody seems to drive a land rover around here."

"Aye, but not all land rovers have a wee royal flag on them, and that one does."

"Oh," said Max.

He wasn't really very interested in the land rover. All he could think about was where to put his 'lost' posters, but he turned around and looked out of the back window. He could see a man who was standing next to the land rover and shaking his head and pointing down the street.

"Is that the driver?" asked Max. "Actually, he seems a bit angry."

"Aye, he does," said Tess.

"Maybe he's just had too much whisky or something," joked Max.

"You're probably right," smiled Tess. "Anyway, let's put one of your posters on the wall outside the post office. It's just around the corner and I can park outside. We'll have to go in and ask first."

"OK," said Max.

Sherlock stopped running and just walked until he saw a fence with a hole in it. He squeezed through the hole and lay on the cool grass under a tree to have a rest. As he panted, Sherlock looked around to see where he was. He was in a field, and in the middle of it there were some sheep that were standing in a small area with a gate and a fence around it. Sherlock sniffed the air and wagged his tail – he could smell the sheep and that was a smell he liked. Just then, he saw a man and a brown sheepdog come into the field and walk towards the sheep in the sheep pen, and then Sherlock heard people clapping. He looked to where the sound of clapping was coming from and could see a large crowd along two sides of the field, but he was more interested in what the man and his dog were doing. The dog sat near the sheep pen, while the man opened the gate. Then the man took a whistle out of his pocket and blew three times. Sherlock watched as the dog went into the sheep pen and ran around the nervous sheep. After a few seconds, the sheep ran out of the sheep pen through the gate and out into the field. The crowd

clapped, and the sheep and the dog ran past Sherlock. Then the man blew his whistle twice and his dog ran around the sheep so that they stopped in a small group and then the dog sat in front of them. The crowd clapped again. The Queen, who was also watching the sheepdog competition from the third side of the field, clapped too, Prince William whispered something in his grandmother's ear, and she nodded.

Sherlock stood up and wagged his tail. The man and his dog seemed to be having a lot of fun, and he wanted to play with them so he ran towards the sheep. The sheep were so shocked that they all ran in different directions. The crowd laughed. The man with the whistle took the whistle out of his mouth. "What's going on? Who does that Sassenach dog belong to?" he shouted.

Sherlock sat down and panted. The brown sheepdog ran towards Sherlock and growled at him and then ran after the sheep. The crowd laughed again. Sherlock wagged his tail even faster and ran after the sheepdog.

The man with the whistle shook his fists in the air. "This is a sheepdog competition and not a circus! Get him out!" he shouted.

The sheep were running all over the field, Sherlock was chasing the sheep and the brown sheepdog was chasing Sherlock. The man with the whistle was chasing Sherlock. The crowd laughed even louder. Even the Queen and Prince William were laughing.

A few minutes later, Sherlock stopped running around the field. He was very proud of himself – he thought he had done a good job: the man with the whistle and his sheepdog were in the sheep pen, and all the sheep were standing around it! Sherlock could hear the loud clapping and cheering from the crowd. Suddenly, somebody he knew was running towards him. It was the gamekeeper! Sherlock didn't wait a second longer. He turned around and ran back towards the trees and squeezed through the hole in the fence again. The gamekeeper stopped in front of the fence and didn't try to follow Sherlock. He just threw his hands up into the air and shook his head. The crowd clapped and cheered even louder as the gamekeeper turned round and walked out of the field.

Max and Tess came out of the post office and heard loud clapping and cheering.

"I wonder what's happening over there?" said Max. "Sounds like a lot of fun."

"Aye, it must be coming from the Games. We can have a look later when we have put all the posters up," said Tess as she put a poster on the wall. "It's good we're allowed to put one here – a lot of people will see it."

"Look there's a newspaper shop across the road," said Max. "Let's ask if we can put a poster in the window."

"That's a great idea." said Tess. "I know the owner, Mr Harris, he's a friend of my father's."

When Max opened the door to the shop, a small bell rang. There were no customers in the shop and there was no sign of Mr Harris. Max and Tess walked through to the back of the shop and found a man sitting behind the counter in a big leather armchair. He was trying to read something on his mobile phone and didn't look up to say hello to them.

"Er, hello Mr Harris," said Tess.

Mr Harris looked at Tess with surprise, got out of his armchair and put his mobile in his pocket. "Hello, Tess. I'm sorry, I didn't hear you come in," he said as he shook her hand. "How are you?"

"I'm fine," said Tess. "And you?

"Not too bad. How's your father? I hope he's well? I haven't seen him for a long time."

"Yes, he's fine. He's busy with his work in Edinburgh, but he's very well."

"Glad to hear it, please give him my best wishes."

"Yes, I will," said Tess.

Max stood on one foot, and then he stood on the other. How long were they going to chat for? He put the posters on the counter with a bang. Tess and Mr Harris stopped talking and looked at him.

"Oh, this is my friend Max," said Tess. "He's from London and he's staying with me and Dad."

"Hello, Max. It's nice to meet you. So you're from London?

"Yes, I am. Could I please put…?"

Mr Harris didn't let Max finish what he was saying. "Life is much faster in London than here, isn't it? Are you enjoying the Highland Games?" asked Mr Harris.

"Well, actually I haven't seen…"

"I wish I could be at the Games instead of working in here," said Mr Harris. "I was just in the middle of reading a funny text message from my wife – she's at the Highland Games – about some kind of wild dog at the sheepdog competition. It sounds like a lot of fun."

Max looked at Tess and then he looked at his watch. "Yes, it does sound fun," he said. "Um, Mr Harris, could you put one of these posters in your window, please?"

"That might be possible. What kind of poster? I hope it's not about a wild music festival in London or something," smiled Mr Harris.

Max gave one of the posters to Mr Harris so that he could look at it. "Oh no, nothing like that," said Max. "It's a 'lost' poster – I've lost my dog Sherlock."

Mr Harris looked at the poster. "That's a lovely picture, and a lovely dog," he said. "I hope you find him. Yes, of course I'll put this in the window for you."

"Thanks," said Max.

"No problem. Is there anything else I can do for you both?"

"No, thanks, I think we should go and put some more posters up in the village," said Tess. "Thanks for you help, Mr Harris. Bye."

"Bye," said Mr Harris.

As Max and Tess opened the door to leave the shop, the little bell on the door rang again. Mr Harris heard the door close and then sat down in his armchair. Just as he closed his eyes to have a little nap, his mobile phone beeped loudly. He opened his eyes and frowned. Then he took his mobile out of his pocket and saw that his wife had sent him another message.

"What does she want now?" grumbled Mr Harris. He opened the message. This time she had sent him a photo with a short text:

Sorry u r in shop + missing fun. Here's gr8 pic of queen + wild dog @ Games xxx

Mr Harris laughed as he looked at the photo. "My goodness, that's the Queen laughing in the background," he said out loud. "That's a great photo." Then he frowned as he looked at the photo more carefully. "That's strange, I've seen that dog before, but where?"

Max and Tess were walking along the street looking for more good places to put up the posters.

"Sorry about that, Mr Harris likes to talk," said Tess.

"Yeah, I thought we'd never get out of there, but it's nice of him to put a poster up."

Just then, Max heard his mobile ring. "Hmmm, I wonder who this is," said Max. "There's no phone number showing."

"Well, answer it numptie, it might be about Sherlock," said Tess.

"Ha, ha, we've only just put some posters up. It's probably somebody trying to sell something. I get calls like that all the time."

"Aye, but don't forget that your mum and my dad have been putting up posters as well."

Just then the phone stopped ringing.

Tess threw her hands up in the air. "Max, you've missed the call?"

"Keep your hair on! Maybe they've left a message."

Just then Max's phone beeped. "See, I told you?" he said.

As he heard the message from the caller who had just phoned, he suddenly became very excited. "It *is* about Sherlock!" he shouted to Tess while he was still listening to the long message.

"See, I told you," shouted Tess. She was now as excited as Max was. "Has somebody found him?"

Max quickly put his mobile back in his pocket. "Not exactly, come on. That was Mr Harris. The 'wild' dog that his wife told him about is Sherlock!"

"But how...?"

"We have to get to the Games as quickly as possible. I'll explain on the way. Do we need to drive there?"

"No, it's just over there," said Tess excitedly. "Come on!"

They quickly ran to the field where the Games were happening. When they got there, Max and Tess pushed their way through the crowd so that they could get to the front and see what was happening. But all they saw was a black sheepdog working with some sheep.

"That's not Sherlock. Where is he?" Max said to Tess. It all looks normal here. Maybe Mr Harris made a mistake..."

"Maybe we should ask somebody."

Tess turned to the man who was standing next to her.

"Excuse me," she said, "we've lost a dog. He's an Old English sheepdog with a tail and we've just got a message that he was running around this field. Did you see him?"

"Oh, so it was your dog that turned the competition into a circus?" said the man smiling. "It was the funniest thing I've ever seen, but you're a wee bit too late, he ran off into the woods."

Max was very excited. "When was that? How long ago? Was he hurt or anything?" he asked the man.

"It was about 40 minutes ago, maybe an hour. And no, he looked fine to me."

Tess quickly took her mobile out of her pocket. "I think we should tell Dad and your mum..."

Max jumped up in the air. "I can't believe it, Sherlock is OK. Now we just have to find him before he gets into more trouble!"

Chapter 7 A strange sound

Sherlock squeezed back through the hole in the fence and ran through the woods until he got tired. Then he walked along the trail by the river until he found a good place to have a little nap. Just as he was about to close his eyes he heard footsteps and a boy and a girl talking. Sherlock quickly stood up and wagged his tail wildly – the boy sounded a bit like Max! Just then, two teenagers with rucksacks on their backs came around the corner and walked along the trail towards Sherlock. He ran up to the boy and sniffed his hand.

"Hey, where have you come from? You're a lovely dog," said the boy as he patted Sherlock on the head.

"Be careful Tim, he's stopped wagging his tail. He might attack you," said the girl.

"No, he's OK, Jenny" said Tim. "I think he thought I was somebody he knew."

"Do you think he's lost or something?" said Jenny.

"I don't think so, his owner is probably somewhere along the trail."

"OK, well, let's find a nice place to have our picnic. I'm starving."

"OK. Bye doggie. It was nice to meet you. Maybe we'll see you again."

Sherlock watched the two teenagers as they walked away from him. Then he went into the wood, where it was cooler, and walked along a little path.

Suddenly, he heard something and stood still. Sherlock looked around and sniffed the air, but he couldn't see or smell anything unusual or interesting like a fox or a deer.

Then he heard the sound again. This time it was a bit louder and longer. Although he had no idea what was making the sound, Sherlock wanted to find out. He lowered his tail and started to walk closer, and very carefully, to where the sound was coming from.

As he got near to a big old tree, Sherlock heard the sound again. This time it was a bit louder and bit strange. All Sherlock could see were two legs on the ground behind the tree. Sherlock went around it and saw that the legs belonged to a man. He was lying on the ground with a whistle in his right hand. Sherlock pushed his cold nose onto the man's face and then licked his left hand. The man couldn't move it but he was able to say two words.

"Get help."

Sherlock understood that the man was in serious trouble. He licked the man's face and then ran back to the river, splashed across it and ran along the trail with his nose to the ground. He could still smell the teenage boy and girl he had met earlier. Sherlock followed their smell until he suddenly saw them sitting down by the river. He went up to them, wagged his tail and barked three times.

"Hello again, doggie," said Tim. "Are you still here?"

"Maybe he really is lost," said Jenny. "He's very wet; he's been in the river."

"Just because he's been swimming, doesn't mean he's lost. It's a hot day and most dogs like to swim. Isn't that right doggie?"

Tim tried to pat Sherlock on the head but Sherlock wouldn't let the boy touch him. He took two steps backwards and barked again.

"What's the matter, doggie? Do you want something to eat?" asked Jenny.

Jenny opened her rucksack and took out a piece of bread and put it in front of Sherlock's nose. "Look, here you are," she said.

But Sherlock wasn't interested in the bread. He took two steps forward and then two steps backwards and barked even louder.

"That's strange. I've never known a dog that doesn't like bread," said Tim. "I think he's trying to tell us something, but what?"

"You've seen too many Lassie films," said Jenny. "Maybe he's sick, you know, with that sickness that makes dogs mad. And then when they bite you, you go mad too. What's it called?"

"You mean rabies. You've been watching too many horror films."

"Well I still think you should be careful."

Suddenly Tim's mobile phone rang. He opened the little phone bag on his rucksack and took it out.

"Oh, no, it's Dad. I suppose I should answer it. How come he always calls me and not you?"

"I don't think he's got my new phone number," smiled Jenny.

"That's clever of you, little sister."

Just as Tim was about to answer his mobile, Sherlock jumped towards him and grabbed the phone out of his hand.

"Hey, give that back," shouted Tim.

But Sherlock wasn't listening. He turned and ran towards the river with the phone in his mouth.

"I don't believe it, what the...?" grumbled Jenny. "You've got to get that phone back!"

"You're right. Come on," said Tim as he stood up and put on his rucksack.

"I'm not going to chase that dog."

"It will be easier if we both try. Look, he's over there, standing by the river. He won't cross it – we can get it from him."

"I can't believe the things I do for you," said Jenny.

She grabbed her rucksack and followed her brother to where Sherlock was standing. The dog looked at them like he wanted to play.

"OK, there's a good dog, give me the phone," said Tim quietly as he slowly got closer to Sherlock. But as the boy's hand almost touched him, Sherlock suddenly turned and ran across the river, splashing water as he went, with the mobile still in his mouth.

"Oh, no," grumbled Jenny. "I don't want to play a game of chase with a dog!"

"I know what you mean," said Tim, "but he seems to know where he's going and I really think he wants us to follow him."

"I'm not sure; maybe we should just let him have the phone."

"Look, we have to find out. Come on. Or do you want stay here?"

"OK, I'll come with you."

Sherlock was already on the other side of the river. He was wagging his tail and waiting for them. The two teenagers crossed the river and followed him into the wood. Sherlock ran through the trees but kept stopping and looking behind him to see that they were still following him. When he got to the injured man, Sherlock dropped the mobile from his mouth and licked the man's face.

14:28

"Good doggie," whispered the man weakly and then he closed his eyes.

Sherlock ran around the other side of the tree. He barked loudly and wagged his tail as soon as he saw the two teenagers running towards him.

Tim got to the man first. He put two fingers on the man's neck to see if he could feel a pulse.

"He looks a bit grey. Is he dead?" whispered Jenny as she stood next to her brother.

"No, there's a pulse and he's still breathing," said Tim.

Suddenly the man opened his eyes again and Jenny gave out a little scream. "Oh, thank god."

"Pain in my chest," whispered the man weakly, "Hard to breathe, feel sick."

"I think you've had a heart attack. Do you think you hurt your back when you fell?"

"Don't think so."

"Good, I'm going to move you so that you can breathe a bit more easily," Tim told the man.

"OK."

Tim carefully rolled the man towards him so that he was lying on his side.

"Do you feel a bit more comfortable?"

"Yeah, thanks."

"What's your name?"

"Ted, Ted Williams."

"OK Ted, don't worry; we'll phone for help now."

Just then Tim saw his mobile phone on the ground where Sherlock had dropped it. He picked it up. "Amazing, it's still working," he said as he dialled 999.

Jenny nodded. She opened her rucksack and took out a little silver packet. Sherlock tried to sniff it.

"It's nothing to eat, it's an emergency blanket," she told Sherlock as she unfolded the silver blanket and carefully put it over the man's body. "It will keep your owner warm."

Sherlock licked Jenny's hand.

"I'm sorry I thought you were just playing a game," she told him. "You're even better than Lassie."

"OK," said Tim as he put his mobile in his pocket and sat beside Ted, Jenny and Sherlock. "A rescue team with a doctor are on their way in an air ambulance. They'll be here very soon, in about 15 minutes or less."

"How do they know where we are?" asked Jenny. "Where's the helicopter going to land?"

"They know exactly where we are because of the signal from my mobile. They're going to land in a small field just the other side of these trees."

"Cool! So now we just have to wait."

"Yep, and you'll wait with us, won't you, mate?" said Tim to Sherlock. "Don't worry; we'll look after your owner."

Sherlock wagged his tail.

"And we'll look after you until Ted gets better," said Max as he gave Sherlock a pat.

"Mum and Dad will kill us!" said Jenny.

"I think they'll be OK about it. It won't be forever, and anyway it's better than putting the dog in a rescue shelter or something. They'll understand. We'll make them understand."

"But what if...?" said Jenny quietly as she looked at the man who had closed his eyes again.

"If what?"

"Nothing, I just hope the air ambulance gets here in time."

Chapter 8 The rescue

After talking to Sir Charles on the phone, Max and Tess agreed that they had put up enough posters in Braemar and that the best thing to do was to buy a couple of sandwiches to eat later, go back to the land rover and drive around near the woods that they knew Sherlock had run into.

"Oh, dear!" said Tess as soon as she turned the key to start the land rover's engine.

"What's the matter?" Max asked her.

"We need petrol or we won't get very far. Sorry about that."

Max looked worried. "Is there a petrol station here in Braemar? I haven't seen one for miles," he said.

"No, there isn't but there's a small one about twelve miles from here," said Tess.

"Will we make it there OK?"

"Yes I think so. It's just that I don't have much cash and they don't take credit cards. But they'll probably let us have petrol because they know me, and they know Dad'll pay them back."

"Wow, that's amazing. That would never happen in London," said Max. "But I've got some money. You paid for our sandwiches, and anyway, I don't want you to pay for all the petrol we're using to find my dog. And, it will probably be faster – we can just fill up and leave."

Tess smiled. "Aye, we Scots can be a wee bit too friendly sometimes."

They drove out of Braemar and about 20 minutes later Tess stopped the land rover in front of a single, old-fashioned petrol pump at the side of the road. The pump looked like an alien from another planet that seemed to be taking in the view over the valley as if it had never seen anything like it before. On the opposite side of the road there was a small house with fields and a Munro behind it.

"This is it," said Tess.

"You're joking," said Max.

They both got out and stood by the petrol pump. Max looked around him in amazement. Next to the little house, behind a stone wall, there were a few scary-looking cows with long horns and long red-brown hair over their eyes.

"This is the smallest petrol station, I've ever seen," he said to Tess.

"We're lucky it's here."

"Is it open? Do we just fill up and go into that little house to pay or what?" asked Max.

Tess pointed to a small sign on the pump. It read:

PLEASE SOUND HORN IF YOU WANT PETROL.

"Wow, I don't believe it," laughed Max. Then he looked a bit worried. "Isn't that a bit dangerous, to press the car horn and make such a loud noise? Those wild animals over there could run over here and kill us with their horns."

"Don't be a numptie," said Tess, smiling. "Those are Highland cows and they might look scary but they are really very friendly. In the old days they were kept downstairs in houses to keep the people upstairs warm."

Max was about to say something about that, when suddenly a woman appeared behind the wall where the Highland cows were.

"Oh hello Tess, it's you," shouted the woman over the head of one of the Highland cows. "Would you like some petrol?"

Tess waved to the woman. "Yes, please, Mrs Andrews," she shouted back.

"I just have to help my husband with the cows, but I'll be with you in a minute. Is that all right?"

Tess quickly looked at Max who was looking at the woman with his mouth open.

"Er, that's fine, we'll wait," shouted Tess.

"I don't believe this," grumbled Max.

"I'm really sorry, Max, but we don't have a choice."

"Yeah, I know. It's not your fault. I'm just worried that if we don't find Sherlock soon, we might never find him."

Tess nodded and then she looked towards the stone wall and smiled. The woman was climbing over it. "Look, here she comes. We'll be on our way again any minute."

Max turned his head and saw the woman walking quickly towards them.

"Great," he said, "and you'll try not to..."

"No, don't worry. I promise I won't let her chat too much," Tess said.

"Oh, I'm so sorry about that, Tess," said the woman as she came up to the pump. "The person who usually helps us is sick, so I have to wear two hats – one for the cows and one for the petrol pump. Shall I fill it up?"

"Aye, please, Mrs Andrews," said Tess. "By the way, you haven't seen an Old English sheepdog around here looking a bit lost, have you? This is my friend Max and he's staying with me and my father, and the dog ran off yesterday while we were walking around Loch Muick."

"No, I haven't, but I'll keep my eyes open," said Mrs Andrews as she started to pump petrol into the land rover. "An Old English sheepdog, you say. There are lots of them around here."

"Yes, but he's got a tail, which is quite unusual," said Max quickly.

"Oh, yes it is. I don't think I've ever seen one with a tail. As I said I'll keep my eyes open."

Tess gave Max one of the sandwiches she had bought earlier and they both ate them as they watched Mrs Andrews fill up the land rover. Suddenly there was a loud noise in the sky that made them all look up.

"Those helicopters are so noisy," said Mrs Andrews as she put her fingers in her ears.

"I hope your cows don't get scared," said Max, finishing his sandwich. He imagined the cows crashing through the wall, then running towards the land rover and turning the three of them into kebabs with their sharp horns.

"Oh, no, they don't get stressed about anything much," said Mrs Andrews.

"That's amazing, because it's flying quite low," said Max as he followed the helicopter with his eyes.

"Oh, I think it's a flying ambulance," said Tess. "I've never seen one of those before."

"No, I haven't either," said Max.

"Well," said Mrs Andrews, "there's probably a climber or a hiker near here, who's had an accident or something. Oh dear. How terrible..."

As the three of them watched the helicopter flying away, Mrs Andrews felt the petrol pump stop.

"Ah, it's full now," she said.

"Great, thank you," said Max as he paid Mrs Andrews for the petrol.

"You're welcome. Hope you find your doggie. As I said I'll keep my eyes open."

"Oh yes, please. Goodbye." said Max. He jumped into the land rover where Tess was already sitting.

Tess waved goodbye to Mrs Andrews and then started the engine. "Let's go back towards Braemar and check out the area around those woods," she said to Max.

"Yes. I'm so glad we're on our way again." Max looked at his watch. "It's amazing," he said. "It's only been 24 hours since Sherlock ran off, but I feel like it's been 24 days."

* * *

"You guys did the right thing, well done!" said the doctor as Ted was lifted onto a stretcher by two other paramedics.

"Is he going to be OK?" asked Jenny.

"Aye, we've given him some oxygen and a drug to help with the pain. We'll do more for him on our way to the hospital. Did you take a first aid course or something?"

"Well," said Tim, "actually I'm in my first year at university and I hope to be a doctor."

"Well, you've helped to save his life," said the paramedic.

"Can we come with you to the air ambulance?" asked Jenny. "It would be great to see it close up."

"Sure. I'm afraid I can't let you come inside though – there isn't enough space and we'll be taking off as soon as possible."

Sherlock walked between the two teenagers as they quickly followed the paramedics to the air ambulance.

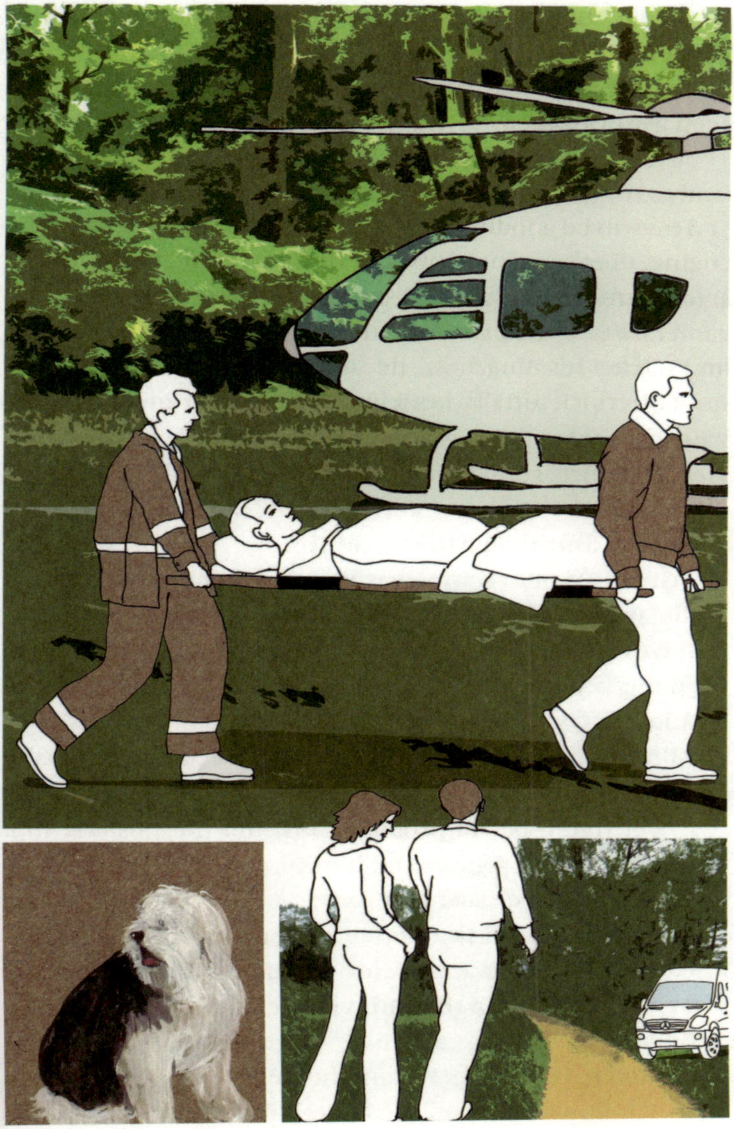

"Wow," said Jenny as soon as she saw the air ambulance in the middle of the field, "how fast do these things fly?"

"About 140 miles per hour," said one of the paramedics.

"Cool! Does one of you fly it or do you have a pilot?"

"We have a great pilot and she's waiting on board."

"Your pilot is a woman? That's really cool!" said Jenny. "I'd love to be a helicopter pilot."

Just then a van with BBC written in large letters on the side of it drove into the field and parked. A man with a video camera and a woman holding a microphone jumped out and started running towards them.

"Oh, it's the BBC news team," said the paramedic. "They were probably in the area because of the Games and saw our air ambulance. I don't have the time to talk to them, but they might want to interview you both. OK?"

"That's fine, it'll be fun," said Tim.

"Great. OK, I'm going to help my team get Ted into the air ambulance. When I give the signal you should move back so that we can take off. So, I'll say goodbye now. Thanks again for doing a great job." said the paramedic as he shook Tim and Jenny's hand.

"I'm glad we could help," said Tim. "Can we call the hospital later and find out how Ted's doing?"

"Aye, that'll be no problem. Just tell the hospital that you're the people who found him."

"Great, thanks," said Tim.

As Sherlock and the two teenagers watched Ted being lifted up into the air ambulance on the stretcher, a few feet away the red light on the BBC video camera was on.

"Are you getting all this?" the reporter asked the cameraman.

"Yep, it's perfect," said the cameraman as he filmed the paramedic, who was standing in the open door of the air ambulance and giving the signal for the group to move back.

"Good. When the air ambulance has flown away, I'd like to interview those two teenagers with the dog."

"OK," said the cameraman.

A few seconds later the blades started to turn and Tim and Jenny waved to the paramedic as the helicopter rose into the air with its lights flashing and then flew away to the nearest hospital.

"Wow, that was amazing," said Tim.

"Yeah," said Jenny. "No one is going to believe this."

"Well, the BBC news people are coming towards us, so maybe we'll be on TV tonight then they'll have to believe us."

"Ha, ha," said Jenny.

"Excuse me," asked the reporter as she came up to Tim and pushed a microphone in Tim's face, "could you tell me what happened?"

"Sure. This dog led us to his owner – Ted Williams – who had had a heart attack in the middle of nowhere," Tim explained.

"So this isn't your dog? That's amazing," said the reporter.

"Yes. It was this dog who saved the man – he led us to him.

"At first we just thought the dog wanted to play with us, but then we knew somehow that the dog was trying to tell us to go with him and help his owner," said Jenny.

"Yeah, he stole my mobile so we had to go after him," smiled Tim as he looked at Sherlock who was wagging his tail.

"Then what happened?" asked the reporter.

"Well, we followed the dog across the river and through the woods and found Ted lying on the ground. He had wandered off the trail. I knew he'd had a heart attack because he looked really grey and had a terrible pain in his chest. My sister and I made him more comfortable and made sure he was warm and then I called 999. The air ambulance came really quickly. They were great," explained Tim.

"This is a great story. Did Ted tell you the name of his dog?"

"Er, no, we didn't think to ask. We were too worried about Ted," said Tim. "Come here doggie; let's see if you've got your name on your collar."

Sherlock came up to Tim and wagged his tail.

"Hmmm, he doesn't have a dog tag or anything," said Tim as he looked at Sherlock's collar. "That's strange."

"Yeah," said Jenny. "I thought that dogs must have their names and a contact number for their owners on their collars – it's the law."

"No problem, I can find that out later. Let's get some shots of the dog by himself," said the reporter to the cameraman.

"OK," said the cameraman as the red light on his camera went off. "Do you just want close-ups or a wide shot as well?"

"Let's do a wide shot as well. It's unusual to see an Old English sheepdog with a tail. Then we can decide in the editing room."

"Is this going to be on TV today?" asked Jenny excitedly.

"Yep," said the reporter. "I think so. I hope it will be on the 6 o'clock news. My producer will like the story because it has a happy ending. TV viewers are so fed up with all the doom and gloom that's happening in the world. Anyway, what's going to happen to the dog? Are you going to take him to a dog shelter or something? Or does the injured man have a family that can look after the dog while he's in hospital?"

Tim and Jenny looked at each other.

"Oh dear," said Tim, "We hadn't thought about that – if Ted's got a family."

"No," said Jenny. "We thought we'd take the dog home with us and look after him until Ted gets better."

"Yeah, but we'll phone the hospital later to see how Ted is, and maybe go and see him tomorrow. Then we can find out more," said Tim.

"Do you live around here or are you just visiting Scotland?" asked the reporter.

"We're on holiday here and Mum and Dad have rented a holiday cottage. They'll pick us up later at the visitors' centre but if we've got a dog with us it might be a bit of a shock for them," said Jenny.

"We haven't even phoned them yet to tell them what's happened," said Tim as he looked at his sister. "Anyway, I don't think the dog will fit in the car!"

"Where are your parents at the moment?" asked the reporter.

Tim looked at his watch. "Well, they are probably at the cottage reading their books in the garden or something boring like that," he said.

The reporter smiled. “Well, I've got an idea,” she said. “We could take you and the dog back to your cottage on the way back to the editing room.”

“Great. Yeah, we'd like a lift. Thanks. I'll call our parents on the way.”

The reporter shouted to the cameraman who was playing with Sherlock: “Have you got all the shots we need of the dog?”

“Yep, I'm ready to go when you are,” he said.

“OK, let's go. We're giving them a lift home.”

“I hope the dog comes with us,” whispered Jenny to Tim. “He might run away or something.”

“I don't think so. He seems to know what's going on. Come on doggie, let's go,” he said to Sherlock.

Sherlock wagged his tail and went with Tim and Jenny, who followed the reporter and the cameraman to the BBC van.

Chapter 9 Sherlock is famous

Max and Tess went into the living room in Sir Charles' cottage. Max threw himself on the leather sofa. "I can't believe it! Sherlock was so near and we drove around for hours and didn't find him," he said. "My mobile hasn't stopped ringing. I've had hundreds of phone calls from people who saw him at the Games, but where is he now! I'm beginning to think that even if Sherlock had a satellite navigation system for dogs, he wouldn't find his way here."

"You can get a sat nav for dogs?" asked Tess. "I didn't know that. That's amazing."

Max looked at Tess if she was from another planet, then suddenly she laughed. "Only joking!" she said as she sat on the sofa next to him.

Max laughed too. "Actually, that would be a really cool invention," he said. "It could tell the dog how far it is to the nearest beach."

"Or to the nearest vet," laughed Tess.

"Or to the nearest dog clothing store with the latest fashion," laughed Max even more. "You know – those jackets that little dogs wear."

"Aye, that would be good; or collars with diamonds."

As they thought of funnier and sillier ideas, Max and Tess laughed and laughed until the tears started to roll down their cheeks. Suddenly the living-room door opened and Mrs Bradley came in.

"Hi you two," she said.

Max and Tess stopped laughing, and then Max and his mother looked at each other without saying anything.

"Er... hello Mrs Bradley," said Tess.

"I didn't mean to interrupt," said Mrs Bradley, "it's nice to hear you both laughing."

"We were just being silly," said Tess. "I think I'll go and make a cup of tea. Would you like one?"

"Not at the moment, thanks," said Mrs Bradley. She sat down in the armchair opposite Max, who was looking at his feet.

"OK," said Tess as she stood up.

After Tess had quietly closed the living-room door and left, Max and his mother sat in silence for a moment. Then it was Mrs Bradley who spoke first.

"Max, I know you think I don't care that Sherlock has run away, but I do care because I know he means such a lot to you."

Max looked at his mother.

"I've been thinking about what you said to me this morning," Mrs Bradley said slowly.

"Mum, I'm sorry about what I said," said Max quickly. "You know, about you being jealous of Sherlock because Dad gave him to me."

Mrs Bradley gave Max a little smile and sighed. "Actually you're probably right. Sometimes I feel you're closer to Sherlock than to me, and you and your Dad were really close to each other. I was always so busy with my work."

Max nodded.

"I miss your Dad too, Max. And I hoped that you and I would be as close as you and your dad were. And I also know that I've been trying too hard to get close to you since he died and that drives you nuts."

Max looked at his mother. She looks so small in that big armchair, he thought to himself. Then he remembered what

Tess had told him about his mother blaming herself about the car accident.

"Mum, can I ask you something?"

"Yes, of course."

Max looked down at his feet for a moment and then at his mother.

"Why didn't Dad drive his car to work on that day? Why did you need to use his car?" he asked very quietly. Max's mother suddenly looked as if she had been hit in the stomach and Max could feel his heart beating very fast.

"Your dad didn't want me to use my car. He thought there was a serious problem with the front wheel. I had a photo shoot that day and I couldn't take my photo equipment on the train..."

Max looked at his mother as she started to cry.

"So it was Dad who..." said Max, who could feel tears coming to his eyes.

"Yes," Mrs Bradley said as she blew her nose. "He suggested I use his car because he could get a lift to work with his colleague."

Max got up and stood beside his mother. He put his hand on her shoulder.

"Mum, why didn't you tell me?"

Mrs Bradley blew her nose again.

"I just couldn't talk about it. But I am so glad we're talking about it now" she said.

"Yes, me too," said Max as he gave his mother a hug.

Mrs Bradley smiled.

"I do care about Sherlock, Max. I really miss that big stupid dog."

"Yes, even I am beginning to think he's stupid," smiled Max.

"I've called quite a few dog shelters this afternoon to see if anybody found him, but no luck."

"Thanks for doing that, Mum."

Just then the living room door opened and Sir Charles came in and stood in front of the fireplace and lit his pipe.

"Oh, I'm sorry," he said, "how rude of me. May I smoke my pipe in here or shall I go outside?"

"I love the smell of a pipe," said Mrs Bradley.

"Yes, me too," said Max.

"That's good to hear. Some people hate pipes," said Sir Charles as he lit it again.

"Dad smoked a pipe sometimes, didn't he, Mum?"

"Yes," said Mrs Bradley as she smiled at Max, "that's probably why we like them."

"Ah, that's right. In fact, I think Andrew and I started to smoke a pipe about the same time. Oh, I mustn't forget to show you those photos of your dad, Max."

"Great. I'd love to see them," said Max. "Would you like to see them too, Mum?"

"Yes, I don't think I've ever seen photos that you took, Charles," said Mrs Bradley.

Just then the big grandfather clock started to ring and Sir Charles looked at his watch. "Goodness, 8 o'clock already. We've missed the 6 o'clock news. Never mind, we can see it later at 10 o'clock if anybody's interested. What about some dinner? Are you both hungry?"

Max and his mother looked at each other and smiled.

"Yes, I'm starving," said Max.

"Good," said Sir Charles, "Mr McDonald has kindly prepared dinner for us and I think we can eat in the dining room in about 15 minutes. Max, could you find Tess and tell her? I think she's upstairs somewhere."

About twenty minutes later, they were all seated around the dining table. Murdo, Mr McDonald's Highland terrier, was sitting under the table just in case somebody dropped a piece of food onto the floor.

"Mmmm, this looks delicious, Dad," said Tess as she took a piece of fish from the big plate in the middle of the table.

"Well, I was worried that Max might not want to eat much so I asked Mr McDonald to prepare something really nice."

"Well, he has. This smells really great," said Max as he took some potatoes from a bowl and then passed it to his mother.

"We've all got to keep our strength up for tomorrow," said Sir Charles, "so we can start to look for Sherlock as soon as it gets light."

Everybody nodded instead of saying anything – they all had their mouths full.

"That picture that Mr Harris' wife took of Sherlock at the Games is amazing," said Mrs Bradley a few seconds later.

"Aye," said Tess, "I'm glad Mr Harris forwarded it to us. I don't think I would have believed him if he hadn't."

"There might be the same kind of picture in the local newspaper tomorrow," said Sir Charles. "I'm sure there were news photographers at the scene."

"Goodness, Sherlock might be famous," smiled Mrs Bradley.

Max smiled too.

"Well, the more people who see his picture, the quicker we'll find him," he said.

"That's true, but most people don't know that he's lost and that we are trying to find him," said Tess.

Suddenly Max's mobile rang. Max quickly took it out of his pocket and looked at it.

"It's Zack," he said, surprised. "That's strange."

"We're in the middle of dinner, Max," said Mrs Bradley quietly. "Could you call him back when we're finished?"

"Yeah, I know Mum, but I think it must be something really important if he's phoning me, he usually just sends text message."

"It's fine with me, Kate, if Max answers it. He could be right – it might be something important," said Sir Charles.

Max looked at Sir Charles and then at his mother, but at that moment the mobile stopped ringing. Everybody at the table was silent.

"Oh, well," sighed Max, "he's probably left a message so I'll call him back," said Max. "I guess a few minutes won't make much of a difference."

Mrs Bradley smiled and nodded. But then Max's mobile rang again.

"Sorry Mum. It's Zack again, I really have to answer," he said as he quickly stood up and ran out of the dining room and into the hall.

"Hello Zack, what's up mate?" asked Max in a worried voice.

"Max, thank goodness you've answered," said Zack on the other end of the phone.

"Yeah, I'm sorry about that. We're in the middle of dinner. Are you OK?"

"Yeah, I'm fine. Listen, Max. I think I've got some news about Sherlock," said Zack.

"What did you say?"

"I said: I think I've got some news about Sherlock."

"Is he... is he dead?"

"I don't think so, mate. Go and have a look at the BBC website. There's a story about two teenagers who rescued a hiker in the area where you are with the help of a dog. There's a picture and I think it's Sherlock..."

Max was so excited that he found it hard to speak. "I'll ... I'll go and look right now and call you back. OK?"

"Yeah, I'll keep my fingers crossed that it really is Sherlock!"

"Zack, you're a star! Talk later. Bye!"

As Max ran back excitedly into the dining room, everybody looked at him. He was jumping up and down with joy.

"What on earth has happened?" asked Tess.

"Sherlock is on the BBC website! Zack has seen him! There's a story about a rescue or something," he shouted.

"What?!" they all said at the same time.

"Sorry Mum, but I have to look at the BBC's website now to see if it really is Sherlock," said Max.

"Er, OK...," said Mrs Bradley as she looked at Sir Charles, who nodded.

"Use my computer upstairs, it's got a bigger screen," he said to Max. "Shout when you have found the story. Go with him, Tess and show him where it is."

Max and Tess couldn't turn on Sir Charles' computer fast enough, and then it seemed to take hours before they were on the BBC website.

"It's not on the main page," said Max nervously. "Where would it be?"

"Hmmm, it's probably under the Scottish news," said Tess.

NEWS
Watch
Sheepdog helps teenage
BACK
1

dog helps teenagers
1
2
3
4

Max clicked the mouse a couple of times and then suddenly he saw a headline that grabbed his attention: **Sheepdog helps teenagers rescue injured hiker.**

"Bingo!" said Max.

In the middle of the report was a photograph of two teenagers and a sheepdog.

"It's him!" shouted Max. "Look, Tess!"

"It is! I don't believe it!"

At that moment, Mrs Bradley and Sir Charles came in to the room.

"Look, Mum! It is Sherlock!" cried Max.

"Are you sure?" asked Mrs Bradley.

"Yes, look! You can just about see his tail. It has to be Sherlock!"

Mrs Bradley looked at the screen more closely.

"I think you're right." Then she started to read the report. "But it says here that the dog belongs to the injured hiker, a Ted Williams."

"But that's not true," cried Max in shock. "It's Sherlock. I know it's Sherlock. What should we do, Mum?"

"I'll go downstairs and call the BBC and see if I can get the phone number of the teenagers or the hiker's family or something," said Mrs Bradley.

"Yes, that's a good idea," said Sir Charles. "Don't worry, there must be an easy explanation to all of this and we'll get to the bottom of it," said Sir Charles.

After Sir Charles and Mrs Bradley had gone downstairs Max put his head in his hands.

"Why do they think that Sherlock belongs to the hiker?"

"Don't worry, Max," said Tess. "Sherlock's been chipped, hasn't he?"

Max looked up at her and nodded. “Yes, that’s proof that I’m his owner.” Then Max looked at his watch. ″I’d better let Zack know that we’ve looked at the website and are pretty sure it’s Sherlock,” he said as he took his mobile out of his pocket.

About 30 minutes later, Mrs Bradley came into the room where Max and Tess were still looking at the computer screen.

“What did you find out, Mum?” asked Max.

“Well, the BBC wouldn’t give me the phone number of the teenager’s parents but...”

“Why not?” interrupted Max.

“For security reasons,” replied Mrs Bradley.

″The person I spoke to said that he would phone the teenagers’ parents first thing in the morning and give them our number.”

“Not until the morning?” asked Max alarmed. “How am I going to be able to sleep tonight?” asked Max.

“I know,” said Mrs Bradley. “But I don’t think Sherlock’s going anywhere tonight.”

“I hope not,” said Max. “You never know what Sherlock will do next.”

Chapter 10 The reward

The next morning everybody was sitting around the table in the kitchen very early. Max yawned. "So what are we going to do while we wait for the phone to ring?" he asked.

"I suppose we could all have another game of Scrabble," smiled Tess.

"What? At 8 o'clock in the morning? We had about a hundred games last night," said Sir Charles.

"And you won most of them, Dad," laughed Tess. "The rest of us have got to have a chance to win some. Would you like another cup of tea, Mrs Bradley?"

"Oh, no, thanks Tess. I feel like I've had a hundred cups of tea since 6 o'clock this morning."

"Well, we can't just sit here," said Max, "although I don't even want to go to the toilet in case the phone rings."

"Aye, I know what you mean," said Tess. "But go to the toilet, and the phone will ring. It's Murphy's Law."

"Murphy's what?" asked Max.

"Murphy's Law. The moment you leave this room, the phone will ring."

"Ha, I bet that's just old Scottish rubbish," said Max.

"Um, it's Irish actually..."

"Well, Irish or Scottish, I'm dying to go to the toilet, so..."

As soon as Max stood up, the phone on the kitchen wall rang. Everybody looked at it and Max quickly sat down again and didn't dare to speak.

Sir Charles picked up the phone.

"Hello?" he said. "Ah, I think you need to speak to Kate Bradley. Just a moment I'll give you to her."

Sir Charles put his hand over the phone. "It's the teenagers' father," he said as he gave the phone to Mrs Bradley.

"Hello?" said Mrs Bradley into the phone. "Yes, it is, that's right, an Old English sheepdog with a tail. Yes, we lost him yesterday while we were walking around Loch Muick. Yes, you must have been very surprised to get a phone call from the BBC. Well, we were very surprised to see him on the website. Could we come and pick him up? We're staying near Balmoral Castle. Yes? That's super."

Mrs Bradley put her hand over the phone. "Can I have a pen and a piece of paper?" she asked Tess.

Tess quickly opened a door of one of the kitchen cupboards, pulled out a note pad and a pen, and gave them to Mrs Bradley.

"OK, I've got a pen now, what's your address?"

As Mrs Bradley wrote down the address, Max tried to read it.

"Is that far from here?" he whispered to Tess.

Tess went around the table to have a look.

"No, it's only about an hour from here," she whispered.

"OK, thank you very much," said Mrs Bradley into the phone. "We'll get there as soon as we can and take Sherlock off your hands. Yes, his name is Sherlock. Oh dear, I'm so sorry. Yes, we'll leave now if that's OK with you. Yes? Good. OK, then. Bye."

Max was looking worried. "Mum, what's the matter? Why did you say sorry on the phone?" he asked.

Mrs Bradley smiled. "Tim and Jenny, or their parents, didn't have any dog food so they gave Sherlock most of their dinner."

"Oh dear, you'd better go and pick him up as soon as possible," laughed Tess.

"You'll come, too, to pick him up, won't you, Tess?"

"Yes, of course, I will, you numptie."

"Can I come as well?" asked Sir Charles. "I wouldn't want to miss this for anything. I can drive us all there, I think I know where they are," he added as he looked at the address that Mrs Bradley had written.

"Great! What are we waiting for? Let's go!" said Max.

About an hour later, Sir Charles parked the car outside a little cottage.

"This is it," he said.

As soon as he turned the engine off, the front door of the cottage opened and Sherlock ran out. Max got out of the car as quickly as he could and Sherlock ran up to him and jumped up, almost pushing Max to the ground.

"Sherlock, get down, you silly dog," laughed Max.

Sherlock covered Max's face with wet licks, and this time, Max didn't care at all. Sir Charles, Mrs Bradley and Tess got out of the car and watched the happy dog and his happy owner for a few minutes. Then they noticed two teenagers who were watching as well. The boy looked a bit sad. Mrs Bradley went towards them.

"Hello, I'm Mrs Bradley."

"Hello, I'm Tim and this is my sister Jenny."

Just then Tim and Jenny's parent's came out.

"Well, he certainly seems to be that young man's dog," said the teens' father.

"Oh yes, that's our Sherlock all right," said Mrs Bradley.

"Well, why don't you all come in and have a cup of tea?" said the teens' mother.

"Yes, I think we've all got a lot to talk about," said her husband.

There weren't enough chairs in the living room, so Max and Tess sat on the floor and Sherlock sat in between them with his head on Max's legs. Tim and Jenny sat on the floor too, while the adults made themselves comfortable on the sofa and armchairs. The teenagers told their visitors how Sherlock had led them to the injured hiker, and the air ambulance had come and then how the BBC news team had interviewed them.

"Wow," said Max. "That's really amazing. Is the hiker going to be OK? What's his name? Ted?"

"Ted Williams," said Jenny. "Yes, he's going to be fine. We called the hospital just before Dad spoke to your Mum, and we actually spoke to him. He told us that Sherlock didn't belong to him. That was really surprising. And then the BBC called and gave us your number. That was even more surprising."

"A friend of mine saw Sherlock's photo on the BBC website. It was part of the report about the rescue," Max told the teens.

"On the website? We saw the report on the local 6 o'clock news on TV," said Tim. "Didn't you see it?"

"No," said Sir Charles, "We missed it."

"It was brilliant," said Tim and Jenny's mum.

"Yes, it was," said Tim. "Anyway, Ted Williams wants to give us a reward for saving his life, but we think Sherlock should have it."

"That's really nice, but Mr Williams doesn't have to give anybody a reward," said Mrs Bradley.

"You're right, Mum, but if Ted Williams does want to give Sherlock a reward, I have a really good idea about what to do with the money," said Max.

"Boxes of his favourite bone biscuits for life?" laughed Tess.

"Close," said Max. "I think the money should go to the homeless people in Edinburgh. Remember that homeless girl and her dog we met, Tess?"

"Oh, yes, her dog was really sweet. The girl was sweet, too. That's a very good idea."

"Yes, so if that's OK with you guys?" Max asked Tim and Jenny.

Tim and Jenny looked at each other and then nodded. "Fine with us," said Tim.

"What do you think, Sherlock?" asked Max.

Sherlock stood up, wagged his tail and then went around to everybody in the room and touched them with his nose. Everybody laughed.

"Sherlock is such a cool dog," said Jenny. "I'll miss him. I wish we could have a dog, but we live in London so it's a bit difficult..."

"London? Cool. That's where I live," said Max, "near London Bridge."

"We live in East Dulwich," said Tim. "So that's not far away from you at all."

"I'll miss you and Sherlock so much ," said Tess. "I hope you'll come up to Edinburgh a lot, there's still so much you haven't seen."

"Oh, yes, we will, won't we Mum?"

Mrs Bradley smiled and nodded. "Of course, we will."

"Oh, by the way," said Max to Tim and Jenny. "Thanks for giving Sherlock a collar. He lost his when he ran away in Loch Muick. Would you like to have it back? It's a really nice one."

Tim frowned. "We didn't put that collar on Sherlock. He was already wearing it when he found us."

"Yes, that's right," said Jenny.

"That's strange," said Max. "I wonder where he got it from."

Max took of the collar from Sherlock's neck and looked at it. His mouth fell open.

"What's the matter?" said Mrs Bradley.

"I don't believe this. There's a coat of arms inside the collar..."

"Let me have a look," said Sir Charles.

Max gave him the collar.

"My goodness," said Sir Charles, "Max is right. In fact, I know this coat of arms – it's from Balmoral Castle."

Everybody looked at Sherlock as if they expected an explanation. He was lying next to Max with his eyes closed, but when he felt that everybody was looking at him, he opened one eye and then closed it again. He was much too tired after his adventure to even wag his tail!

Vocabulary

A

AA (automobile association) Automobilclub *(wie ADAC in Deutschland)*
abseiling Abseilen *(Bergsport)*
alarm alarmieren
alright in Ordnung
amazed erstaunt
amazement Erstaunen
attention Aufmerksamkeit
aye ja *(besonders in Schottland gebräuchlich)*

B

backwards rückwärts
bang (n+v) Knall; knallen
bark bellen
battle Kampf, Schlacht
bench Bank
bend (n+v) Kurve; biegen
belt Gürtel
beside neben
bet (n+v) Wette; wetten
blade Rotorblatt
bone Knochen
bonnie hübsch *(besonders in Schottland gebräuchlich)*
boot *hier:* Kofferraum
breathe atmen
burp (n+v) Rülps; rülpsen

C

care about sth./sb. etw./jdn. wichtig nehmen
carry tragen
cash Bargeld
certainly sicherlich
chase (n+v) Jagd; jagen
cheek Wange
chest Brust
Christmas Weihnachten
clothing Bekleidung
coal Kohle
coat of arms Wappen
collar Halsband
colleague Kollege
cottage Hütte, kleines Landhaus
counter Theke
countryside Landschaft
cover bedecken
couple of ein paar, zwei
crash (n+v) Krach, Unfall; abstürzen, krachen
crown Krone
cruel grausam
cry (n+v) Ruf; weinen, rufen

D

dare (n+v) Herausforderung; wagen
dial wählen
diamond Diamant
dog biscuit Hundekuchen
dog tag Hundemarke
doom and gloom Unheil und Trübsinn
door knocker Türklopfer
drive sb. nuts jdn. wahnsinnig machen

drug Droge, Medikament
dry **trocken**

E

earplugs Ohrstöpsel
editing room Schneideraum
emergency Notfall
engine Motor
entertainment Unterhaltung

F

fast train Schnellzug
fault Fehler, Schuld
fence Zaun
fill füllen
fireplace Kamin
first aid Erste Hilfe
flag Fahne
flap (n+v) Flügelschlg; flattern
flash (n+v) Blitz; aufleuchten, vorbeirasen
forward (adj. +n) vorwärts; weiterleiten
fresh frisch
frown (n+v) Stirnrunzeln; die Stirn runzeln
fur Fell, Pelz

G

gamekeeper Wildhüter
ghost Geist
god Gott
grave Grab
growl knurren
grouse Moorhuhn
guy *ugs.* Typ

H

headline Schlagzeile
headphones Kopfhörer
heart attack Herzinfarkt
hiker Wanderer
hike (n+v) Wanderung; wandern
horn Horn, Hupe
howl (n+v) Heulen; heulen
hug (n+v) Umarmung; umarmen
human (adj. +n) menschlich; Mensch

I

I'm starving *ugs.* Ich bin am verhungern
in case falls
injured verletzt
instead dafür, stattdessen
interrupt unterbrechen
invention Erfindung

J

jewel Juwel

K

keep sb. posted jdn. auf dem Laufenden halten
keep one's hair on ruhig bleiben

L

law Gesetz
lead *hier:* Leine
lick lecken
lie down Platz! (Befehl für Hund)

lift (n + v) Aufzug, Mitfahrgelegenheit; heben
light (n + v) Licht; beleuchten
lit up beleuchtet
lovely hübsch, reizend
low niedrig
lower senken

M

master *hier:* Herrchen
motorbike Motorrad
motorway Autobahn
mouth (n + v) Mund; Worte lautlos mit den Lippen formen
my goodness meine Güte

N

999 Notrufnummer *(wie 110 oder 112 in Deutschland)*
nap (n + v) Nickerchen, Schläfchen; schlummern
neck Hals
nerves Nerven
notice (n + v) Notiz; bemerken
nowhere Nirgendwo

O

order *hier:* bestellen
out of breath atemlos
oxygen Sauerstoff

P

pain Schmerz
pant hecheln, keuchen
pat (n + v) Klaps; tätscheln
paw Pfote
pee pinkeln
pen Pferch, Stift
petrol Benzin
press drücken
prison Gefängnis
protect beschützen
pump (n + v) Pumpe; pumpen
puppy Welpe

R

rabies Tollwut
reach erreichen, reichen
rescue (n + v) Rettung; retten
rescue centre Rettungsstelle
reward Belohnung
rocket Rakete
roll rollen
roller coaster Achterbahn
rise, rose, risen aufsteigen

S

satnav Navigationsgerät
scream (n + v) Schrei, schreien
screen Bildschirm
seat (n + v) Sitz; setzen
second Sekunde
secret Geheimnis
sense Sinn
serious ernst
services *hier:* Raststätte
sewage Abwasser
shake, shook, shaken schütteln, wackeln
shall sollen
shelter Asyl
shield Schild
shoot schießen
sheepdog Hütehund

sick krank, übel
sigh (n+v) Seufzer; seufzen
since seit
skin Haut
snail Schnecke
sniff schnüffeln
spare keys Ersatzschlüssel
speed Geschwindigkeit, Tempo
splash (n+v) Spritzer; platschen
steep steil
strength Kraft
stretcher Trage
such so
swan Schwan
sword Schwert

T

tag Marke, Schild
tail Schwanz
tall groß
tear Träne
though aber, jedoch
thought Gedanke
throw up sich übergeben
tissues Taschentücher
tongue Zunge
traffic light Ampel
trail Pfad, Wanderweg
turn sth into sth. etw. in etw. verwandeln

U

unusual ungewöhnlich

V

van Lieferwagen, Transporter
vacuum cleaner Staubsauger
vet Tierarzt
viewer Zuschauer

W

wag wedeln
warning Warnung
wear two hats zwei Rollen spielen
wee klein (besonders in Schottland gebräuchlich)
wet nass
wide shot Totale
windscreen wiper Scheibenwischer
wing Flügel
wipe abwischen
wish (n+v) Wunsch; wünschen
wonderful wundervoll

Y

Yuck! *ugs.* Igitt!

Gaelic words

Auld Reekie (Old Smokey) [ˌɔːld 'riːki] gälischer Name für Edinburgh
Dinna fash yerself! (Don't worry!) ['dɪnə faːʃ jɛːrˌself] Keine Angst!
kilt [kɪlt] Kilt, Schottenrock
loon [luːn] Bengel, Bursche
Munro [mʌn'ro] Berg
numptie ['nʌmpti] Idiot
Sassenach ['sæsənæx] Engländer
sporran ['spɒrən] Felltasche
toonser (townser) ['tuːnsə] Stadtmensch

Reading tasks

Chapter 1

1 Do you like to go on trips with your parents? Why/why not? Why does Max think the trip to Scotland is going to be horrible?

2 What do you know about Sherlock? For example, what is one of his favourite things to do?

3 How does Max feel about his mother? Describe their relationship.

Chapter 2

1 What happened to Max's father?

2 Find a Scottish phrase and two Scottish words in this chapter and explain what they mean.

Chapter 3

1 In this chapter Max meets Tess. Does he like her? Why/ why not?

2 What do you learn about Edinburgh? What would you like to see first on a sight-seeing tour?

3 How are the lives of Maggie and Sir Charles different?

Chapter 4

1 Max thinks it would have been worse if Sherlock had thrown up on Tess. Why does he think that?

2 What's the Gaelic word for 'idiot'?

3 What's the longest walk you have been on and where?

4 Why did Sherlock run off into the woods?

Chapter 5

1 Why is it important that Max's poster has a picture of Sherlock that shows his tail?
2 Why do you think Mrs Bradley was upset that Max didn't use one of the photos she had taken of Sherlock?
3 Do you find it easier to talk to a good friend about a problem than to a parent? Why/why not?

Chapter 6

1 Most pets don't like to go to the vet. Why do you think that is?
2 What do the owners and their dogs have to do at a sheepdog competition?
3 What do we learn about Max when he is in Mr Harris' shop?

Chapter 7

1 Do you know what to do if somebody has an accident and needs help?
2 Why do Tim and Jenny think Sherlock belongs to Ted?
3 Have you ever had to help someone in an emergency? If so, what happened?

Chapter 8

1 What do you think Tess meant when she said that Scots can be a bit too friendly sometimes?
2 Why does Max feel it's been 24 days since Sherlock ran off and not 24 hours?
3 Were you surprised that the air ambulance pilot was a woman? Why/why not?

Chapter 9

1 Why did Tess go and make a cup of tea when Mrs Bradley came into the living room?

2 Why was everybody silent when Max's mobile stopped ringing?

3 Why does Max have to wait until the next morning before he can see Sherlock?

Chapter 10

1 Why did Tim look sad when Max arrived?

2 Will Tim and Jenny see Sherlock again?